# WHAT ARE THEY SAYING ABOUT
# SCRIPTURE AND ETHICS?

# What Are They Saying About Scripture and Ethics?

*William C. Spohn, S.J.*

PAULIST PRESS
*New York/Ramsey*

IMPRIMI POTEST
John W. Clark, S.J.
October 12, 1983

Library of Congress
Catalog Card Number: 84-60732

ISBN: 0–8091–2624–9

Published by Paulist Press
545 Island Road, Ramsey, N.J. 07446

Printed and bound in the
United States of America

# Contents

Foreword     1

Introduction     3

1. The Command of God     19

2. Scripture as Moral Reminder     36

3. Call to Liberation     54

4. Response to Revelation     70

5. Call to Discipleship     89

6. Scripture as Basis for Responding Love     106

Epilogue     129

Notes     137

Suggested Readings     146

*[handwritten annotations: "Class Viewpoint", "up to here for Test #1"]*

# Foreword

When theologians turn to Scripture for moral guidance they are not acting like moral philosophers. They turn to a history rather than a theory of ethics, to a canonical text whose credential is inspiration by God and not merely logical consistency. Christians turn to Scripture to discover more than the right thing to do; they want to act in a way that responds to the God of their lives. Systems of ethics begin with a fundamental principle or value. The Gospel begins with a person who claims that he himself is the "norm" we are to follow: "Come, follow me."

In both the Hebrew and Christian Scriptures a way of life is presented to God's people to follow. That way of life is inseparable from the history that has revealed their God. Using Scripture in Christian ethics, therefore, must be rooted in that history and the One it reveals. The theologian faces a host of questions that need not bother the philosopher: What texts are central to this way of life? How are they to be interpreted in light of what we know about God and Christ? What are the morally revealing dimensions of biblical symbols, narratives, parables, poems, and how do they color our reading of the rules and principles in Scripture? No wonder that theologians have a lot to say about using Scripture in ethics. Even less surprising is the lack of agreement among them.

In the chapters that follow we will examine six typical ways that Christian theologians are employing Scripture in ethics. I hope that this will lead the reader to discover some of the richness that biblical studies have made available to Christian ethics. The field of ethics in the latter part of the twentieth century is beginning to assimilate the advances made in biblical scholarship in the past century. This is a particularly fruitful time for Christian ethics and should lead to a richer appreciation of Scripture for all believers. Every form of biblical literature, from love poetry to parable, evokes a response to God and to others. The text does not lead us into a faithful way of life; that is the accomplishment of God's grace. But the text can alter our vision and our feelings, our characteristic ways of acting and evaluating so that we respond more fully to the One the Bible reveals.

I am grateful to the theologians who have enhanced my reading of God's Word; to my students who challenge me to understand it anew; to my friends and colleagues, especially at the Jesuit School of Theology at Berkeley, who call me to be faithful. Special gratitude goes to the Jesuit community at the University of Santa Clara and the Louis Bannan S.J. Foundation whose generous hospitality during 1982–83 made this work possible.

# Introduction

What are theologians saying about Scripture and ethics? All sorts of things—not all of which can be fit into one systematic approach. Six different ways of using Scripture for moral guidance emerge from reading the wide range of theological positions. These six approaches form the six main chapters of this book. This pluralism is a sign not of scholarly chaos but of the irreducible richness of Scripture itself. Believing that four Gospels are better than a single one, the Church welcomed pluralism even in its most central document. Both our moral life and the range of literary forms in the Bible are simply too rich to be reduced to a single moral system.

Let us briefly discuss our original question. We will look at *theologians* writing about *ethics*. The origin of theology and its practical test must always be rooted in the experience of believers. The task of theologians is to put lived experience of people of faith into organized terms. Ethics is the more organized and abstract expression of morality, our ordinary experience of discovering what is worth living for and trying to live for it. Morality and the life of faith are the actual lived experience; theology and ethics are the attempts to examine that experience and organize that experience in a more abstract way to enhance the moral life and the life of faith.

We will study the use of Scripture *in ethics,* a different task than that of studying the ethics in Scripture. The scholarly examination of the ethics of Paul's epistles or the influence of Judaism on the Sermon on the Mount must be presupposed here. What we are asking is what bearing the moral teaching of Paul has today on us as citizens. Does his advice in Romans 13:1–7 counsel us to adopt a passive attitude toward state authority because it is "ordained by God"? And while it is important to know what the Matthean communities understood by "turning the other cheek," our task here will be to determine what that phrase means for Christians caught in the nuclear arms race. Inevitably we will ask questions of a classic text that the author could not have foreseen, and that text can provide answers beyond its author's original intentions. A text is a classic that speaks in the voice of one culture to a more universal human audience in subsequent cultures. The Christian belief that the same Spirit that inspired the authors of Scripture still inspires the use of Scripture in the Church today gives us hope of a faithful continuity with those early believers.

The meaning of a specific scriptural passage *then* has a controlling influence on its meaning *now*. "It is a general rule of proper textual interpretation that a text should be read for what its author meant to say and what its first readers or hearers would have heard it say," writes John Howard Yoder, one theologian we will consider.[1] Nevertheless, he applies scholarly conclusions on the text's original meaning to situations the biblical authors could not have anticipated. As we shall see, this problem is two-edged: almost every author justifies the *now* meaning of Scripture he or she proposes by claiming that it is closest to the *then* meaning of the original setting.

### Pluralism in Scripture and Ethics

My basic point is that we enjoy an irreducible plurality of theological uses of Scripture in ethics because of the irreducible plurality of literary forms in the Bible itself. For example, the Bible contains, among other forms, both commands and stories. There are accounts of God calling people, from Abram and Sarai to the disciples by the Sea of Galilee. Our first group of theologians views this sort of encounter with God as the model for Christians' continuing relation with him. God commands and we obey. We need to unearth the theological reasons for such a selection, namely that God is primarily sovereign Lord and that existential decision is key to the moral life. Another set of authors, however, choose narrative material as the key literature for ethics. The Bible guides our journeys, they say, by the stories of faithful people who have journeyed with God, culminating in the story of Jesus' journey, which led to the cross. Stories are different from commands—they have a different impact on us. A good story induces us to reflect on ourselves and ask deeper questions about who we are and where we are going. A command, on the other hand, does not invite reflection but orders us to act. Choosing either stories or commands as more fundamental for ethics needs to be justified by theological argument.

The main difficulty in fundamentalist as well as mainstream use of Scripture is the tendency to treat the Bible as a book of rules. Applying Scripture to ethics is immediately narrowed if we view ethics as mere rules and Scripture as a collection of moral norms. I recall a book from the library of our seminary entitled *The Divine Armory of Sacred Scripture*. In it, the Word of God was portrayed as a quiver of quotations to be drawn in moral and doctrinal argument. Although that book was more than fifty years old, many preachers even today take a moralistic tack with the Word of God on Sunday mornings. They distill a moral "lesson" from the readings, which forms the basis of the weekly harangue. Or else they wrench a line from its scriptural context as a "proof-text" for a moral stance that was actually formed on different grounds.

Scripture is too rich a document to be used as a quarry for moral lessons. It is a whole library of books rather than a single book, a rich display of the variety of expression of cultures centuries apart. The Word of God employs many ways of telling us who we are and what we are called to become. Every book of the Bible has a moral aspect to it, but moralizing is the least helpful way of presenting that aspect. It takes both faith and imagination to understand that the exodus from Egypt is about our life today, that the historical account of David concerns anyone who lives richly before the Lord, that the prophetic denunciations speak to today's adulterous generation as much as to Jeremiah's contemporaries. The Psalms are lyric expressions of our own praise and lament and they form the dispositions of our hearts even as we pray them seriously. If we are insensitive to the special dynamics of lyric poetry, however, we may ask: "What's the point?" The lyric of "walking through the valley of the shadow of death" then becomes a prosaic message about patiently enduring daily irritations. Even those passages of direct moral prescriptions, such as in the second half of many of Paul's letters, lose their impact when divorced from the theological proclamation of what God has done for us. How many times do we read the Ten Commandments and omit the historical prologue that makes them a covenant response rather than a mere code of laws? The whole story of Sinai and the introductory words, "I, the Lord, am your God, who brought you out of the land of Egypt, that place of slavery" (Ex 20:2) precede the Decalogue's proclamation. The call of covenant morality rests on profound gratitude for an undeserved deliverance. Since that gratitude empowers faith-filled obedience, omitting the Exodus story impoverishes our response to the Decalogue.

**Morality Is More Than Rules**

Our own moral experience is also too rich to define morality as a simple set of rules, even if they do play an indispensable role in any morality that aims to be practical. How do we decide what to do when faced with a major decision in our lives? Rules are not the only sources of insight we have in deciding about a career change or the level of income to which we aspire. We gradually discover our way by sorting through our own remembered experiences, seeking advice from friends, looking to the example of people we admire, considering the commitments we have already made and the people who depend upon us, using our imaginations to envision the kind of people we would become in certain possible environments. We might also consider the state of the world today, a world of scarcity for some and surplus for others; we would probably spend some time quietly and prayerfully sorting out our reactions to possible courses of actions. We might consult the example of Jesus to see where the path of discipleship is leading. We might even discuss possible choices with some trusted and wise figures in the Church community. In a word, the voice of conscience is like a chord that unites a wide range of tones into a harmony. Merely asking "What must I do to keep the rules?" hardly does justice to our rich moral experience. If God's Word is to speak to the complexity of this experience, it must have an equally rich number of avenues of expression. Hence, it is no wonder that an appreciation of Scripture for moral guidance will begin by admitting that the whole range of literary forms found in the canon addresses us morally.

Ironically, both fundamentalists and overly secularized Christians misuse Scripture by treating it only as a book of rules. Fundamentalists believe that the revelation of God is exactly the same in any part of the Bible; they thus claim to be able to take any verse and, without further interpretation, apply it as a moral guideline for today's Christians. Fundamentalism is a theology masquerading as an anti-theology. Lacking any critical awareness, it takes a particular form of nineteenth century American theology for granted and claims that this theology is actually the literal, plain sense of Scripture. When fundamentalism is not critical of its own presuppositions and methods, it often smuggles the values of bourgeois prosperity and nationalism into its use of Scripture. When it rules out any form of moral guidance for the Christian other than its own reading of the Bible, it is systematically immune to criticism. A modern example of this literal interpretation of the Bible and the resistance of fundamentalism to criticism is the racial prejudice that still exists in the South. Ordinary human decency and the consensus of the American judicial system cannot dissuade some colleges from forbidding interracial dating. At Bob Jones University, such a rule is not admitted as vestigial segregationist prejudice, but justified as the clear command of  God from the Old Testament. Other preachers of the New Right assure us that supply-side economics is the plain will of God, invoking the New Testament's statement that those who do not work ought not to eat (see 2 Thess 3:10). Contrary to fundamentalist practices every scriptural passage needs interpretation, and every honest theology admits its method openly.

On the other side of the spectrum are those who contend that Scripture has no real authority for believers today. They argue that the cultural distance of our own society from societies that practiced holy war, child sacrifice, subjugation of women, or public execution by stoning is too vast to salvage any moral role for Scripture. If historical criticism has demonstrated how the various portions of Scripture were formed and reformed for particular communities, what possible lasting inspiration can the text offer us today? Instead of trying to interpret this outdated document, the Church should look elsewhere for insight on our own pressing issues, most of which were not even remotely anticipated by the authors of Scripture.

The preceding is in part an argument against authority, a theological matter that each of the six approaches to Scripture we will consider must explain. In general, we can say that Scripture is normative for Christians because the risen Lord of faith is identical to the person who was crucified, Jesus of Nazareth. Christians believe that the definitive, though not the exclusive, revelation of God occurred in the life of Jesus. Hence, the testimony of the first Christians to Jesus is the privileged revelation of the reality of God. God's intentions for human living are revealed through the whole of the canonical Scriptures, and not simply in archaic norms. Ironically enough, to reject the continuing moral authority of Scripture on the grounds that many of its moral rules are outdated is to err on the same grounds as the fundamentalists: both arguments treat the Bible primarily as a book of rules. In both cases, the prevalent wisdom of a particular culture becomes morally authoritative, unchallenged by the Gospel that cannot be cozily accommodated to any culture, liberal or conservative.

Within more mainstream Christianity, two further theological tendencies have restricted the use of Scripture in Christian ethics. The first is the Reformation warning on the role of morality in relation to salvation. Martin Luther and John Calvin detected the danger of legalism in paying excessive attention to morality. The second is Roman Catholic moral theology which has depended so heavily on natural law as the source of moral teaching that Scripture is either an afterthought or merely an ornament to a philosophical treatise. Before giving an overview of the six models, let us examine why both of the major branches of Western Christianity have been reluctant to use the Bible as a guide for life.

### Legalism: The Problem of the Latent Pharisee

Part of Martin Luther's legacy to mainstream Protestantism is a suspicion of the Law in relation to faith. Luther saw in the self-concern of many Christians about their own perfection a dynamic that Paul had denounced. In his Letters to the Galatians and Romans, Paul insisted that the Law, though given by God, could never be salvific. The Law points out our transgressions but cannot save us from them. Its true function is to lead us to despair of trying to earn our salvation from God. The Gospel saves us from this self-centered preoccupation by relocating our trust in the gracious power of God, freely given in Christ. The Gospel is good news because it saves us from a commercial relationship with God in which we try to oblige God to reward our moral accomplishments with his grace.

Law precedes Gospel in the experience of justification in Christ, but justification does not terminate Law in our experience. So long as we are both flesh and spirit, we will always know the temptation to "works' righteousness," the tendency to impress the Lord with our good deeds. In the spirit there is freedom, but in the letter of the Law we will find death. Hence, even faithful Christians are ambivalent toward moral norms. We need such norms to order society and point out transgression, but they appeal to the latent Pharisee of our flesh.

In his writings on the Decalogue Luther insists that the first command that calls us to faith is the indispensable precondition for keeping the other commandments. Unless our trust shifts from our own efforts to the grace of God, we will use each commandment as a rubric for our own righteousness. It will be too easy to claim that we have kept the Law only because we have not committed adultery or murdered anyone. Luther reinterprets the Decalogue to take away any grounds for boasting. He changes these norms into commands about virtuous attitudes and dispositions, which must continue to grow and can never rest in self-satisfaction. Commenting on the prohibition against killing, he writes,

> Not only he who directly does evil breaks this commandment, but also he who unnecessarily omits a service to his neighbor which he might render by anticipating and restraining, and by protecting and rescuing his fellow man from bodily harm and suffering. The chief design of God is that we permit no injury to befall any person, but that we show to everyone all kindness and love.[2]

We can never say, "I've loved enough; I've shown enough kindness." By turning the norm into a command regarding disposition, Luther removes from the Law its tendency to make us boast of our accomplishments before God.

This legacy has left many Lutherans ambivalent toward the issue of morality. The normative passages of Scripture become particularly difficult to interpret, since they seem to contain some threat of legalism. Even an appeal to follow the Sermon on the Mount or other explicit calls to discipleship runs the risk of presenting Jesus as a moral teacher rather than a bearer of God's free gift. John Calvin acknowledged a more constructive role for moral reflection in the Christian life; he saw it as a guide and source of encouragement in living out the grace of justification. Even the most morally earnest of Reformed Christians like the Puritans, for example, tended to translate scriptural guides for action into commands about dispositions of the heart. In our first model, "The Command of God," we shall see how the Lutheran Dietrich Bonhoeffer and the Reformed Karl Barth have reinstated the normative aspect of ethics and still maintained the primacy of Gospel over Law.

### Does Natural Law Need Scripture?

Roman Catholic moral theology has traditionally found its basis in natural law, a philosophical ethics, rather than in Scripture. According to such philosophy our ordinary human experience can instruct us on what we need to do and not do. Wherever human beings are found, certain necessary moral patterns rest on their common humanity; natural law is the reasonable expression of these common human necessities. As John Macquarrie states, "Natural law is foundational to morality. It is the inner drive toward authentic personhood and is presupposed in all particular ethical traditions, including the Christian one."[3] Our humanity is not a blank slate on which anything at all can be written; certain kinds of behavior lead to human flourishing while others lead to human frustration. This is true for all, Christians and non-Christians alike.

What can Scripture offer if morality is already established by nature? It cannot provide us with new content for morality, new information that human reason could not itself discover. Scripture could publicize to a fallen humanity what would otherwise be more difficult to know, and it could provide new motivation to do what is naturally right. However, in the actual instruction of moral theology and in the "manuals" or handbooks used in seminaries, Scripture played a minimal role. Even in the papal social encyclicals of the last hundred years, scriptural quotations are only occasional ornaments to supplement philosophical argument about the rights of labor or the duties of the state. Only after the Second Vatican Council do the official teachings of the Roman Catholic Church employ biblical imagery and themes. In a positive sense, this natural law tradition can speak to anybody of good will by appealing to the humanity that believers and non-believers alike possess. On the negative side, it does not nourish the moral reflections of believers on the profound realities of grace, freedom, and the person of Christ, which are the wellsprings of Christian commitment.

It is not surprising, therefore, that one of the Vatican Council's major requests in revising the training of priests should be a plea for a more biblical moral theology:

> Other theological disciplines should also be renewed by livelier contact with the mystery of Christ and the history of salvation. Special attention needs to be given to the development of moral theology. Its scientific exposition should be more thoroughly nourished by scriptural teaching. It should show the nobility of the Christian vocation of the faithful, and their obligation to bring forth fruit in charity for the life of the world. . . .[4]

In the second chapter, we will see how moral theologians since the Council have responded to this invitation and still maintained a natural law foundation. While Protestant moral reflection has stressed the realities of Christian conversion to the possible detriment of normative material, Roman Catholic moral theology has shown great confidence in applying moral rules to situations but neglected the transformation of heart that is central to New Testament moral teaching. Since Bernard Häring's landmark work, *The Law of Christ,* and Josef Fuchs' *Natural Law,* Catholic theologians have worked to redress this imbalance and show that Christian responsibility can be grounded in a biblically informed natural law.[5] Such Protestant theologians as James Gustafson, Paul Ramsey and others responded to the challenge of situation ethics by spelling out the necessary function of moral norms in Christian morality, but not by resting those norms on a natural law philosophical foundation.[6]

Let us now take a brief look at each of the six models for the use of Scripture in ethics. Naturally, these are not hermetically sealed compartments. While each model tends to concentrate on a specific form of biblical literature as the primary means God uses to reveal his moral intentions, all of the models refer to other forms of expression as well. Consequently, overlapping of the models is inevitable. This schema is intended as a pluralistic framework to highlight the pluralistic possibilities for using Scripture. The fifth model will present my views as a supplement to the previous positions, rather than as a refutation.

## The Command of God

The first model, like each of the others, answers the basic moral question, "What ought I to do?" Its distinctive approach states: "Listen to the personal command of God directed to you and respond in obedient faith." This model focuses on those passages in Scripture that describe God's call to specific individuals and makes them the paradigm for all subsequent moral interaction.

With this approach, the Bible does not present us with general moral principles which we then apply to our situation. Any statements that seem to be general principles such as the Decalogue are actually mere summaries of God's call to specific individuals. At best they set the boundaries for the community of the covenant, the limits of life acceptable to God. They are like the white lines at the outer edge of a highway warning drivers to stay on the road. Like the lines, they cannot teach the motorists how to drive on the road. Life is guided within these boundaries by the direct, personal and specific inviting commands of God to individuals.

Just as Jesus called his disciples with a direct authority that could be met only by unquestioning obedience or disobedience, the demands of that same Lord call Christians of every age to become his disciples. The person who would stop and try to analyze philosophically that call to discipleship has already begun to hesitate and disobey. To have faith means to be obedient, and only those who do obey the costly demands of the Lord actually have faith.

The obvious problem is how to recognize God's call. What dispositions of heart will enable us to discern the actual command of God? What qualities experienced by the listening believer indicate that a specific sense of obligation actually comes from God? Fundamentally, we turn to Christ for this discernment: only commands that witness to Christian freedom, which are calls rooted in the saving gift of Christ, can come from God. And only if we are guided by the Spirit of Christ can we obey with the joyful freedom of his disciples.

## Scripture as Moral Reminder

This model is that espoused by modern proponents of natural law Christian ethics. What ought I to do? I must be human because the Lord has embraced that humanity in the incarnation. Scripture presupposes natural moral law and human ability to know what is right and wrong. God's intentions are already inscribed in our human nature in the dynamic drives to human flourishing and our intelligence, which orders those drives. Even though sin has clouded our motivations, it has not totally obscured our capacity to recognize the moral law.

As Thomas Aquinas taught, the New Law of Christ is primarily the gift of the Holy Spirit and secondarily the written letter of the Law.[7] Christ *does* bring a new dimension to the moral life, but it does not consist in new information about what it means to be human. It lies rather in this gift of the Spirit, which transforms our motivation so we can live the moral life with spontaneity and joy. In fact, any seemingly distinctive commands of Christian ethics, even if they are not always recognized as such, are already part of human morality at its deepest level.

For example, some people have asserted that the radically distinctive character of Christian ethics can be found in the commandment, "Love your enemy." They assume that at best, pure natural ethics could tolerate enemies out of consideration for their humanity. Josef Fuchs, however, points out that this command was always part of natural morality. If it were not, then it must be permissible for non-believers to hate their enemies![8] Rather than seeking new commands in the Bible, Christians should look for the witness to the fundamental reorientation of their basic intentions toward God. Only the grace of Christ can provide this radical conversion of heart.

## Call to Liberation

From the experience of Latin American churches and the movements of human liberation, such as the civil rights movement and the feminist struggle, a third model for the use of Scripture emerges. Christians must join the oppressed in their struggle for liberation because only there can God be found. Scripture is used in a complex fashion here, combining some of the elements of the fourth and fifth models with an historical and economic analysis of the situation. The key symbol and event that reveals the God of Israel is the exodus from the slavery of Egypt. The Old Testament's historical and prophetic literature makes clear that God acts for the oppressed and demands the same commitment from those faithful to the covenant. Jesus confirms and deepens this liberating action of God by his own ministry, which challenged the oppressive, unjust structures of his own day.

Although liberation theology does not identify political liberation with the coming of God's Kingdom, it sees an indispensable connection between the struggle for justice and God's freeing us from sin. Since sin is embodied primarily in social structures, no real conversion can occur without first changing those dominant structures. All of the moral imperatives of the New Testament must be interpreted in light of this struggle. If my enemy is a military dictator, I can only "love my enemy" effectively if I struggle to remove the very power by which he oppresses other people. Hence, armed revolution cannot be ruled out by any literal appeal to the Sermon on the Mount.[9]

## Response to Revelation

Our fourth model turns the moral question around. The Christian should ask "What is *God* doing in my life?" before asking the question "What ought I to do?" The basic imperative, therefore, is "Respond to the one God who is acting in everything that is happening to you." This approach presumes that God is intimately involved in the actual patterns of history and culture as well as the events of our personal lives. He does not direct everything that occurs, as in the old doctrine of predestination, but in a more complex way he judges, redeems and creates in history.

H. Richard Niebuhr, the American Protestant theologian, in the middle of the Second World War, asked: "What is God doing in the War?"[10] He searched the Bible for perspectives that would enable him to discern the hidden action of God in the present tragedy. He used the biblical symbols of judgment and the crucifixion to interpret the suffering of the innocent. Niebuhr did not claim any direct pipeline to the mind of God, but he did apply some basic patterns of God's action in biblical times to detect how God was acting in the war. These perspectives can help illuminate the present situation so that the believer may find the One who still acts in character today. Niebuhr concluded that God was endorsing neither side but was judging both the Allies and the Axis for their sins and calling all to repentance. The Bible continues to provide resources that allow us to discern God's present action and determine a fitting response.

### Call to Discipleship

*Authors emphasis is on this chapter.*

In our fifth model, moral questions are answered by referring directly to the New Testament story of Jesus Christ. To be disciples, Christians ought to embody their Master's distinctive way of life. The most important literary expressions here are story and parable. The story of Jesus claims to be the truth of our lives, so we either have to let it redefine our own identity or dismiss that claim as false. Prior to questions of action is the question of character. Do we have a coherent sense of self at the core of our identity? Unless the Gospel story redefines the person's character, he or she cannot follow the way of life proper to the disciple.

Letting the story of Jesus serve as the pattern for our own lives will conflict with the basic assumptions of our secular culture, which has its own story, one quite different from that which should be lived out in the Christian community.

For example, in Stanley Hauerwas' opinion, the abortion debate is like a spoken conversation between two deaf persons; neither side can enter the other's universe of discourse. Pro-life forces object to abortion on the basis of philosophical convictions rather than explicit

Christian grounds. Pro-choice arguments are rooted in the secular story of our liberal culture, which maximizes choice and personal autonomy. The actual question the Church should pose is not whether the fetus is human, but whether the fetus is a child. Christians have to examine what kind of people we must be to welcome children into our communities as gifts, not threats.[11]

### Responsive Love

This final summary position owes much to the previous models. It takes the new commandment of Jesus in John 15:12, "Love one another just as I have loved you," as the answer to the moral question. This mandate, spoken at the Last Supper after the washing of the feet, defines the Christian moral life as one of response and imitation. The love that Christ commands has a definite shape to it, a shape learned only from the experience of actually having been loved by Christ. The present experience of believers is normatively formed by the New Testament witness of Jesus and the whole story of God's dealings with Israel. Each virtue of the Christian life refers in some way to this pattern of God's love and finds as its motivation a grateful response to that enduring love.

This is an ethics of imitation, but not of the externals of Jesus' ministry. Rather, the locus of transformation is the heart of the Christian, where the fundamental dispositions and deep emotions that link conviction and action are shaped. The Spirit works to sanctify Christians by developing in them virtues and dispositions that correspond to those manifest in the historical Jesus who is the risen Lord. These cannot be abstracted from the biblical testimony. For example, when Paul exhorts the community at Philippi to consider each other's needs ahead of personal interest, he urges them to have the same attitude as Jesus. He then recounts in a beautiful hymn how Christ emptied himself even to the cross for us and how God raised him up. That faith memory provides not only the motivation for placing others first, it also shapes the content of true Christian altruism in community. Because the love that is at the core of all virtues of the Christian life has this same fundamental pattern, each of those virtues can be understood only in reference to the biblical testimony of how that distinctive love first appeared.

Some readers will find one of these six approaches more congenial than the others. The particular religious traditions that have influenced our interpretations of the Scripture may make some biblical literature more accessible to us than others. For other readers, several approaches described here will be familiar, which indicates that their own reading of biblical literature has already used several avenues of expression for moral reflection. Our aim is to place a fuller range of biblical material before all readers so that the discernment of the community will be enhanced by the richness of God's word.

# 1
# The Command of God

The faith history of Israel begins with a call that reveals Yahweh and demands a simultaneous response from Abram. The mysterious presence summons the latter to leave his ancestors' land and all that is familiar to him to "go to a land that I will show you" (Gen 12:1). A similar call inaugurates each of the great epochs of Israel. A reluctant Moses is called to lead the people out of slavery by a Lord who will accept no excuses. The prophets speak with the authority of Yahweh because they have been summoned personally. Jesus proclaims the Kingdom as a reality that claims the lives of his hearers; some leave everything behind to follow him while others, like the rich young man, turn away.

Our first approach to the use of Scripture for moral guidance uses this experience of divine summons as the paradigm for the Christian's relation to God. God's self-revelation is always a personal claim on those who witness it. In all situations of moral decision, God is the commander and the believer is the one commanded. The moral question "What ought I to do?" is answered by listening in faith: You should listen to God's command and then obey it unquestioningly.

The paradigm of command emerged most clearly in the neo-orthodox movement, which sought to sever the compromising alliance of Protestantism with modern culture and revive the faith's biblical foundation. Among the movement's leading figures were Karl Barth and Rudolf Bultmann, and the younger theologian who studied under them, Dietrich Bonhoeffer. We will first examine Bonhoeffer, who laments the problem most earnestly, and then investigate the writings of Bultmann and Barth for philosophical and theological rationale in this use of Scripture.

## I. Dietrich Bonhoeffer: The Cost of Discipleship

Dietrich Bonhoeffer's writings gain credibility from the remarkable life he led that produced them. He wrote *The Cost of Discipleship* in 1938 at the age of thirty-one. At the time he was a professional theologian and rector of a seminary for the Confessing Church, which opposed the Nazi-dominated German National Church. He would later be imprisoned by the Nazis and executed at the age of thirty-nine on the grounds that he was involved in a plot to assassinate Hitler. Bonhoeffer is perhaps best known in America for his *Letters and Papers from Prison,* which describe his struggles during the final months of his life.[1]

Bonhoeffer staunchly resisted the complacency of European Christianity, especially as exemplified in the silence of the German church. He presented a challenging vision of Jesus' call to radical discipleship, which demanded wholehearted obedience to the way that leads to the cross. His writings continue to influence Christians today, particularly those groups, whether Catholic charismatics or socially active Evangelicals, that want to make a clear distinction between the Church and secular culture. *The Cost of Discipleship* recaptures the simple directness of Jesus' invitation to his disciples and asserts that the same invitation is extended to us today. The first time Jesus confronts an individual with the demand to leave his or her former existence and pursue an uncharted path forms the paradigm, the normative pattern, for the rest of the journey. "Jesus' summons to the rich young man was calling him to die," writes Bonhoeffer, "because only a man who is dead to his own will can follow Christ. In fact every command of Jesus is a command to die, with all our affections and lusts."[2]

The initial summons to discipleship and the Sermon on the Mount are vivid examples because they honestly and poignantly set the terms for the most costly of journeys, the one that leads to death on the cross. A modern Christianity too comfortable with the betrayals of its culture resisted this radical tone. Bonhoeffer reprimanded his fellow Lutherans for their misunderstanding of the relationship between Law and Gospel, between faith and works. Originally, "law" was interpreted as any use of good deeds to attempt self-justification before God, but its legitimate function of guiding obedience in faith had all but disappeared. Bonhoeffer certainly agreed that faith came only by accepting the free gift in Christ, the gracious promise of the Gospel. Martin Luther had not hidden the call present in the promise, the call to live out the Gospel by being other "Christs" to the neighbor.[3] However, he struggled more with the lazy believers who used "evangelical freedom" as an excuse to rest on their laurels of justification than he did with the legalists who preoccupied him in his early writings.

Bonhoeffer calls the moral inertia of Gospel without Law "cheap grace" and contrasts it with the costly grace of true discipleship. "Such grace is *costly*," he writes, "because it calls us to follow, and it is *grace* because it calls us to follow *Jesus Christ*."[4] Cheap grace absolves sins without asking repentance and enables the Christian to be perfectly at home in the world, even the world of Nazi Germany.

How can we recapture the legitimate urgency of Gospel obedience without falling into the trap of legalism, which tries to purchase God's favor with good works? We must discover a more integral connection between Law and Gospel. When Jesus Christ calls, it is a gracious event that transcends any distinction between Law and Gospel. He summons us to exclusive attachment to his person; it is thus a gracious summons, not a legal imperative. Nevertheless, that allegiance to Christ is impossible without obedient action: "Christ calls, the disciple follows, that is grace and commandment in one,"[5] writes Bonhoeffer. The encounter with the rich young man in Matthew 19 shows this connection. Jesus is not interested in the man's moral quandaries, but in the man himself. When confronted by the summons to discipleship, the young man and all of us face a yes or no choice. Only if he is obedient and follows Jesus down the road can the man enter into that relationship with Jesus in which he may  know the mercy and graciousness of God. The young man does have a choice; the call does not suspend his humanity. His obedience will be the first step of faith. He must not wait until he has "sufficient" faith before being obedient; he must take the step. And there is the tragedy: "Because he would not obey, he could not believe."[6]

We delude ourselves if we think we must develop more faith before answering the call. "Only he who believes is obedient," states Bonhoeffer, "and only he who is obedient believes."[7] Bonhoeffer relishes paradox as much as Luther did. The excuse of insufficient faith is actually a posture of no faith at all, and much of our morally earnest questioning is an attempt to dilute the radical summons of Jesus. Moral clarity is not a pre-condition of discipleship. In fact, the journey is uncharted, as was Abram's; the wandering Aramaean did not know where he was being led, only that he was being led. Jesus stands between the disciple and the command because his life interprets the command, and it is his personal authority that summons the disciple. We do not follow Jesus because the command is an attractive prospect for personal fulfillment or reward—that would put the command between Jesus and the disciple. Unquestioning obedience is possible only because it is the trusting assent of faith in the One who is unconditionally trustworthy.

## The Cross of Christ as Moral Standard

Every Christian ethics is a careful balance of several components, usually around one dominant theme. In Catholic moral theology, that primary strand was traditionally the natural law philosophical explanation of morality. We will see that the doctrine of God dominates Barth's ethics. James Gustafson showed in his *Christ and the Moral Life* how various Christologies have guided the major thinkers in the Christian tradition.[8] Different aspects of belief in Christ become central in indicating the moral response of the Christian. For Bonhoeffer, the cross is the true measure of Christology in ethics. Jesus is the image of God, the standard for humanity that overrules any philosophical definition. Nothing is more revealing of Christ than his sufferings, nothing more definitive for the way of discipleship. "Just as Christ is Christ only in virtue of his suffering and rejection," writes Bonhoeffer, so the disciple "is a disciple only in so far as he shares his Lord's suffering and rejection and crucifixion."[9]

The cross is the sign of contradiction, which revolutionizes all our personal values and projects. Each value must be submitted to the unique historical standard of the cross and resurrection of Christ to determine its actual meaning. We cannot presume to know from human standards what God is doing in Christ, as Bonhoeffer eloquently argues in his *Ethics*. He comments on the verse "God is love" from the First Letter of John 4:16:

> First of all, for the sake of clarity, this sentence is to be read with the emphasis on the word God, whereas we have fallen into the habit of emphasizing the word love. *God* is love; that is to say not a human attitude, a conviction or a deed, but God Himself is love. Only he who knows God knows what love is; it is not the other way round; it is not that we first of all by nature know what love is and therefore know also what God is. No one knows God unless God reveals Himself to him. And so no one knows what love is except in the self-revelation of God. . . . Only in Jesus Christ do we know what love is, namely in His deed for us. "Hereby perceive we the love of God, because He laid down His life for us." (1 John 3:16)[10]

How does the New Testament answer the question "What is love?" It points to the saving deed and person of Jesus Christ. He is the only standard that matters.

Although the person of Christ is central to this schema, discipleship does not necessarily imply literal imitation of his public ministry or his poverty. Such literalism would itself be an evasion of radical obedience to the call. We can hide behind the biblical text to avoid God's living word that commands us anew. For subsequent generations of Christians, the call to discipleship is contained in their baptismal vocation. In *The Cost of Discipleship,* Bonhoeffer comments first on the Sermon on the Mount and then on the missionary discourse of Matthew 9 and 10 to delineate the original call. He then derives much of the same moral message from Paul's theology of baptism and its consequences. These are the continuing sources of the Gospel imperative for us. Bonhoeffer does not expect special revelations from the Holy Spirit to communicate particular commands to us. "If we would hear his call to follow," he writes, "we must listen where he is found, that is, in the Church through the ministry of

Word and Sacrament. . . . If you would hear the call of Jesus, you
need no personal revelation: all you have to do is hear the sermon
and receive the sacrament, that is to hear the gospel of Christ crucified and risen. Here he is, the same Christ whom the disciples en-
countered. . . ."[11] As in the writings of the other proponents of the
command of God, the metaphor of hearing is central: it is not the
disciple's responsibility to figure out how to follow, but only to hear
and obey wholeheartedly.

## II.   Rudolf Bultmann: The Crisis of Decision

In his *Jesus and the Word,* Rudolf Bultmann presents a similar
ethics of faithful obedience combined with indefinite content. In this
book, written in the 1920's, Bultmann, whose extensive writings on
the New Testament set the course for twentieth century exegesis,
draws out the moral implications of his method. It is as much a polemic against every sort of ethics as it is a presentation of a biblical
alternative. Every attempt at ethical theory threatens idolatry because ethics stands between the Christian and the direct, concrete
call to unquestioning obedience spoken by Jesus.

Surprisingly, Bultmann refuses to let even the biblical text provide the content of the divine command. He does this for theological
and philosophical reasons, which determine his interpretation of
Scripture. Every theologian is guided by some convictions about God
and the human agent, but few are as explicit as Bultmann in admitting them. For him, existentialist philosophy is the key to theology
and to an accurate grasp of Scripture. God is radically Will, "the
Power who constrains man to decision."[12] At the core of human reality is the bare necessity to make a decision, because we become someone definite only through free commitment. No commitment means
there is no authentic person, only an irresponsible object. Even in the
murky light of ambiguity and personal anxiety, we are constrained to
choose. We all face the radical temptation to pass off our responsibility of free decision to external determining forces of circumstances,
institutions or authority figures.

Jesus understands that in the present moment we are faced with
this necessity to decide, and his proclamation of the imminent coming of the Kingdom vividly portrays that necessity. "If men are

standing in the crisis of decision," writes Bultmann, "and if precisely this crisis is the essential characteristic of their humanity, then every hour is the last hour. . . . Thus he understood and proclaimed his hour as the last hour."[13] The demanding will of God confronts us anew at every moment, in every concrete situation, in every place where this crisis of decision is found.

If we examine the actual requirements that Jesus articulates, we are liable to miss the radical call of God. Our conduct will become something separate from us; we will delude ourselves into thinking that God wants some sort of work from us when in fact he demands not a deed but our very selves. Ultimately, every moral claim is the fundamental claim of faith. "Altogether the will of God is complete obedience," says Bultmann, "surrender of one's own claim."[14] We can thus understand why Jesus taught no ethics as understood in the ordinary sense of a rationally grounded system of values and obligations. His only concern was to confront each person with the radical either/or—total trust in God's grace or seeking our selves. When we focus on the particular moral imperatives of the New Testament, we are covertly attempting to reduce this absolute demand for obedient faith to relative demands for obedient behavior.

God's demands are intrinsically intelligible and inherent in the present situation. Hence, "man is trusted and expected to see for himself what God commands."[15] Beyond this, Bultmann offers nothing more specific. Listening to the text rather than to the living God can lead to disobedience. "Whoever appealing to a word of Jesus refuses to dissolve an unendurable marriage," he writes, "or whoever offers the other cheek to one who strikes him, *because* Jesus said so, would not understand Jesus. . . . All these sayings are meant to make clear by extreme examples that it is not a question of satisfying an outward authority but of being *completely* obedient."[16] The Christian must be disarmed even of moral principles in this lonely confrontation with God. Turning to ethics evades hearing the present call of God.

The controlling ingredient in this interpretation of Christian "ethics" is existentialist philosophy. The discipline has often been conceived of as a theological enterprise consisting of four components: Scripture, theological tradition, philosophical ethics and pertinent empirical data. Frequently, one of these components is the controlling element in a given thinker's reflections on Christian ethics, and in Bultmann's case it is existentialism. It controls his reflections and determines his interpretation of New Testament material. Moral philosophies typically present a normative view of humanity, some notion of appropriate human living to guide our actions. Paradoxically, existentialism offers a non-normative view because it disallows moral principles as threats to human authenticity. This philosophy reinforces the Lutheran suspicion of Law. It combines theology and philosophy to offer a unique reading of the New Testament. (The aversion of existentialism to finding moral content in the sayings of Jesus is puzzling. The Gospels seem to imply his seriousness about selfless service, indiscriminate love and other moral issues. They do not read as mere examples of the extremity of existentialist faith commitment.)

Although Bultmann adamantly refuses to fill in the normative void of the divine command, Bonhoeffer seems to have moved in just that direction. In his *Ethics,* he clarifies how the Christian should respond to the call of discipleship by referring to the claims of family, civic and vocational responsibilities. In traditional Lutheran theology, these "orders of creation" had functioned as provisional indications of the will of God. In this fallen world, God wills that we respond to the demands of family, state and vocation, at least to prevent social chaos. They are never direct media of God's will, however, since they are inevitably tainted with sin. Even in *Ethics,* Bonhoeffer reduces every moral choice to a question of radical faith or radical refusal. The absolute demand for surrender in faith overshadows and may even forbid any positive role for ethical clarity. Even if one agrees that our moral choices are not in themselves salvific, we still need to clarify what we are to do and who we are to become through our choices.

Karl Barth retains in principle this theological and philosophical polemic against moral philosophy but modifies it considerably in practice. In sorting out such moral issues as abortion, war, and capital punishment, he parallels Bonhoeffer. On theological grounds, he must thunder against the dangers of ethics for the believer, but to be practical he shifts to a form of moral generalization to clarify where one can expect to find the command of God. This double-minded method may argue the necessity of some normative view of humanity in Christian ethics; even though it may be banished as theologically suspect, such a view must be restored, at least in part, when the theologian deals in practicalities.

## III.  Karl Barth: The Command of God

Karl Barth offers the most developed theological rationale for using Scripture as the command of God. Through strenuous ecclesiastical and political efforts, as well as his monumental *Church Dogmatics* (written from 1925 to 1955), Barth strove to redirect the course of Protestant Christianity in this century. Although as a student he had completely accepted the blend of Christian faith and German humanism propounded by his masters, he became disillusioned with this alliance at the outbreak of World War I. When almost all of his mentors abandoned their socialist and pacifist principles to line up with the Kaiser and German nationalism, the young Swiss was scandalized. Their political collapse proved to him that their theological foundations were bankrupt. Even among his pastoral colleagues, he realized that "everything, above all everything that has to do with the state, is taken a hundred times more seriously than God."[17] The young Reformed pastor was overwhelmed by a desire to rediscover "the Godness of God" and find ways to speak about God that were not compromised by worldly allegiances.

In his groundbreaking *Epistle to the Romans* and the numerous volumes of *Church Dogmatics,* Barth adopted the theological method he found in Luther and Calvin.[18] He returned to the plain sense of Scripture and articulated dogma in service of preaching the Gospel. Like the reformers, he eschewed any dependence on philosophy to back up his theology. Any such alliance would only make the Gospel the lesser partner and reduce it to the wisdom of the current culture. Instead, Barth made the doctrine of God central to dogmatics and the theological ethics it contained. His ethics are found in three major sections of the *Dogmatics,* and in each the ethics are carefully subordinated to the theological doctrines. In II/2, he considers the election of God and its corollary, the command of God. In III/4, under the title "The Protection of Life," he analyzes the various issues of life and death as consequences of the doctrine of creation. Finally,

in IV/2, the doctrine of the reconciliation of Christ sets the context
for the love command and the specific demands of Christian discipleship. They are the concrete dimensions of justification and sanctification. His method is obvious from the order of the topics: the theology
must control the ethics because Christian moral action is fundamentally an active and grateful response to what God has done for us in
Christ.

*Law: The Claim of the Gospel*

Before we examine the actual use of Scripture as the command
of God, we must develop Barth's theological foundations of Christian moral life. He revolutionized the traditional Protestant reading
of Law and Gospel by inverting the two so that the order is "Gospel
and Law." Law neither precedes Gospel nor is an obligation tacked on
to it. "The Law is completely enclosed in the Gospel. It is not a second thing alongside and beyond the Gospel," writes Barth. "It is not
a foreign element which precedes or only follows it. It is the claim
which is addressed to us by the Gospel itself, and as such, the Gospel
insofar as it has the form of a claim addressed to us, the Gospel
which we cannot really hear except as we obey it."[19] If we know the
grace of God, we will also experience the sovereignty of God over
our conduct. Either we acknowledge this Lordship or we do not
know the grace of Christ. Law is the form of the Gospel, whose content is Christ. This claim is intrinsic to the saving events: morality is
our joyful correspondence to the action of God in history. Our conduct must conform to, witness and imitate the victory of Christ. The
whole witness of Scripture thus determines the content of Christian
ethics because every dimension of theology will have its corresponding moral claim. The call is inseparable from the gift.

Barth employs the metaphor of command and divine Commander to describe the claim of God's sovereign election upon the
believer. Humans are confronted by an alien word that interrupts
their ordinary lives and demands obedience to the Commander. The
one who receives a command does not have to inquire about its content. Such inquiry would be the beginning of disobedience. The metaphor implies the directness of hearing a definite word, and the moral
qualities that are praiseworthy are attitudes leading to prompt and
wholehearted obedience. These commands of God are not general

moral principles founded on human nature or observation of experience. They are as immediate as the spoken word.

No mediated or mere natural origin for the moral claims we experience could account for their inherent qualities of unconditionality, goodness, definiteness and the like. Barth insists that the only basis for these qualities of the moral demand is that it comes from the divine Commander. No ethics that is less than theological can account for these qualities. The moral demand is unconditional because it comes from an unconditional source. Indeed, every quality of the moral demand points to the same source. For example, the content of the moral demand is not in itself *good* but has a borrowed goodness from the One who speaks it. Again, "the whole singularity and uniqueness of God as the Lord," writes Barth, "is reflected in the particularity of what He wills and commands. . . . The command is always the particular decision and disposition, and therefore the particular revelation, of this supremely particular Commander."[20] Therefore, we can discern which demands are from God because their inherent qualities refer us back to their divine source. They are unconditional, majestic, right, good, personal, definite, eternal and unifying because God is all these in his action. He meets us in the event of his command.

These commands are not bolts out of the blue, says Barth, but rather "the claim of God's command always wears the garment of another claim."[21] Obligations bombard us daily, and we must discern which of these are actually from God by attending to the type of claim they make upon us. The Christian is not a passive receptor but an active discerner of the divine command cloaked in daily obligations. Although he enumerates with his characteristic amplitude a long list of qualities that are signs of the divine claim, Barth does offer two principal signs:

1. The divine command is permission before it is command. The central sign should correspond to the central quality God has manifested in history, namely, graciousness. Divine commands will be experienced as positive gifts rather than obligations. Barth writes, "The form by which the command of God is distinguished from all other commands . . . consists in the fact that it is permission—the granting of a very defi-

nite freedom."[22] Commands that are not from God bind us
and we experience their bidding as essentially forbidding.
Gracious permission grants us the freedom to *be* in a specific
direction, and therein lies the command's enabling power.
Barth often insists that our may is our must. "This is the case
because the command is itself the form of the grace of
God."[23] The Law indicates the direction that the gift of freedom must take because ruling grace is commanding grace.
But it is always grace first and foremost.

2. The divine command always directs us toward imitation of
Jesus Christ because he is the pre-eminent and definitive
manifestation of God's grace. We are commanded to take the
right *attitude* toward him, says Barth, "with the faith and
love and hope which all have in Him as their ground and
content."[24] Like Bonhoeffer and Bultmann, Karl Barth is
wary of specifying the content of Christian ethics; instead he
points us to the formal pattern of Christ's life. We are to imitate Jesus in the attitudes of our response rather than in
copying the details of the historical Jesus' lifestyle. The basic
pattern for imitation is found in the Christological hymn of
Philippians 2. Christians are to imitate that attitude present
in the self-emptying of Christ. "What is required of us,"
states Barth, "is that our action should be brought into conformity with His action."[25] The point of contact is the attitude more than the specific action. Because our own
imitation will always be conditioned by sin, we can never
boast of perfect conformity to Christ.

*Witnessing in Action the Attitude of Christ*

The biblical norm for Christian action is the overall witness of
Scripture, which provides the formal pattern for Christian response.
This witness also specifies the attitudes that shape true obedience.
Barth turns the content question "What are we to do?" back into a
formal question that is a religious matter first and a moral one second. What seems to be a question of content is actually one of religious assent in faith. "The obedience which the command of God
demands of man," Barth writes, "is his decision for Jesus Christ. In

each individual decision it is a special form, a repetition and confirmation of this decision."[26] The rich man of Mark 10 disobeys the call to faith by concentrating on the moral content of the external command. Confident that he has done God's will because he has kept the commandments, he is actually evading the more radical claim. "It is required that he should let himself be loved," Barth states. "This is the demand to which he is not equal, to which he is disobedient. . . ."[27] Barth seems to presume that the content of a particular divine command will be evident in the event of its being spoken. Prior speculation about the content is superfluous.

The paradigm of command and Commander is the key to interpreting the commands and norms of the Bible. Ethics errs by interpreting the Decalogue or Sermon on the Mount to be instances of more general human obligations as though lying were immoral because it destroys social trust. Such general natural obligations cannot reflect the uniquely personal God who intervenes in human history. Even when we find biblical norms expressed as general obligations, we should read them as summaries uniting many particular commands into a comprehensive demand.  Even the Decalogue cannot be reduced to generalities. It delineates the boundaries of the life of God's people like a fence enclosing a field. Each commandment is a summary of what God has consistently addressed to his elect. Action beyond these boundaries is known in advance to be inconsistent with the One who established the covenant of grace. "God will command and forbid within these limits and not elsewhere," states Barth.[28]

The sovereign free God is not programmed merely to repeat these directives. The faithful person must listen for a command that will be unique and specific to his or her situation. The believer, however, does not stand in an historical vacuum. Even though the biblical commands were addressed to particular people of a different time, this does not diminish their continuing relevance for us today. "As God speaks in the events of these summaries," explains Barth, "He will always and in all circumstances speak to each individual."[29] Barth asserts both the uniqueness and the consistency of the divine command without any careful attempt to reconcile them. God is both unique and consistent, and his commands must therefore also reflect these qualities.

Barth's theology provides a reading of the Sermon on the

Mount similar to that of the Decalogue. He writes, "Now it is Jesus Himself (as once the God of Moses) who defines, in the form of comprehensive positive and negative directions, the sphere in which He is present with His own, with those whom He has called and will call, the sphere of His care for them and lordship over them."[30] The arduous demands of the Sermon are only appreciated and gratefully received if we accept them as notification and description of the new life possible in Christ. They seem arduous only if our attention is self-centered, if we focus on our own capacities for turning the other cheek or loving indiscriminately those who cannot repay us. Barth dismisses, somewhat grandly, such doubts about our capability. "The limit of their capacity becomes irrelevant," he states, "when that which Jesus the Lord accomplishes for them occupies the center of the picture which is a norm for their own life's picture. . . . Grace itself decides what is natural in its own sphere."[31] Our limits do not determine the extent of God's renewal; a new humanity is present in Jesus Christ. Our call as found in the Sermon on the Mount is merely permission to confirm in our lives the pattern of that new humanity.

Scripture, therefore, provides *summaries* of God's commands, *attitudes* that should inform our obedience, and *directions* of freedom inherent in the gift itself. The whole of Scripture provides the testimony to which our lives should correspond, but the specifics of that correspondence will be determined by the mundane daily obligations which cloak over God's command. Those that manifest the qualities shining out from the events of salvation will reveal the Commander behind his gracious command. In language subsequent chapters will employ, the "story" of Scripture provides the normative framework to hold in proper balance the various attitudes and directions that guide obedience to the divine command.

## Respect and Protect Life

One test case for Barth's ethics is the divine command to respect and protect life, which he discusses in *Church Dogmatics* III/4. Does he relegate the moral agent to the "wastelands of relativism" by banning any general moral principles? We shall see that the "prominent lines" of God's commanding turn out to be fairly definite. Even while he maintains his polemic against ethics, which is an evasion of the particular command of God, Barth does outline moral norms and their legitimate exceptions on questions of abortion, suicide, capital punishment, self-defense, war and mercy killing.

Before describing the Law concerning the protection of life, Barth proclaims the divine gift: now we *may* respect life. "The real truth is not that we must live," he states. "It is that we may live. Life is the freedom which is bestowed by God."[32] The doctrine of creation teaches that life is a blessing, a loan from God of something belonging to God. Consequently, the claim of Law inheres in the theological content of the Gospel: we must treat our own existence and that of others with respect and joy. General responsibilities come with our humanity because we are free to exist in this particular, that is to say, human, structure. Because they share a common species, different human beings will hear analogous divine commands. "What God says to him applies to him," says Barth, "but to him only as a creature that has others of his kind."[33] We are created for freedom in fellowship with others as well as with God; hence social obligations come with this gift. Human life, however, does not have value in and of itself. The command of God creates respect for it. "Respect," says Barth, "is man's astonishment, humility and awe at a fact in which he meets something superior—majesty, dignity, holiness, a mystery which compels him to withdraw and keep his distance, to handle it modestly, circumspectly and carefully."[34] Here, as elsewhere, every moral value is immediately dependent upon God's worthiness.

### Moral Norms in God's Command?

This theology provides the interpretation of the commandment "Thou shalt not kill." It is directed against murder, not against any taking of human life. He can state the norms for deciding life and death issues. Each of these norms except killing the weak has legitimate exceptions: against this there is an exceptionless prohibition— God would never command it. Human reflection is a necessary prelude to hearing the command of God in each situation, presumably even if this reflection yields moral principles. The judgment of God decides, states Barth, "which in the last analysis we must all hear in every actual or conceivable situation after considering the human arguments on both sides."[35] This listening does not prevent Barth from performing some of the very casuistry on moral questions he had earlier derided.

The command to protect life usually forbids taking life in abortion, but not always. "Let us be quite frank," writes Barth, "and say that there are situations in which the killing of germinating life does not constitute murder but is in fact commanded."[36] The reasons for the exceptions are clearly stated. Each exceptional abortion is a genuine option for the protection of someone's life threatened tragically by the life of another.

Killing in self-defense remains highly suspect due to the Gospel prohibitions against it, which clearly bind the Christian to greater respect for the opponent's life than what is required naturally. Although we should not adopt, like Tolstoy or Gandhi, an absolute prohibition against killing in self-defense, Barth admits that they are closer to the direction of Jesus' attitude than "the primitive gospel of the mailed fist and all the doctrines that have tried to blunt the edge of these sayings." The New Testament sayings on non-resistance do not merely "constitute a special rule for good or particularly good Christians. They declare the simple command of God which is valid for all men in its basic and primary sense, and which is thus to be kept until further notice."[37]

Tyrannicide and capital punishment for high treason during wartime are the only exceptions to this prohibition. Barth wrestles with the case of his friend and former student, Bonhoeffer. How could a Gospel pacifist be justified in plotting to kill Hitler? If the plotters had received a clear command from God, why were they unwilling to act in full disregard for their own lives? From the outside, Barth cannot resolve the issue except to comment: "The only lesson to be learned is that they had no clear and categorical command from God to do it. Otherwise they would have had to overcome what was not in any case an ethical difficulty. . . . In such a situation it might well have been the command of God. For all we know, perhaps it was, and they failed to hear it."[38] Such are the difficulties in this model of ethical intuitionism: in difficult cases, only those who hear the command can know whether an action is justified or not. No amount of explanation to others or investigation of the results can indicate whether they were acting morally or not.

In the final section of his theological ethics in IV/2 of the *Dogmatics*, Barth shows again that he is more willing than Bultmann to set down definite attitudes and even norms for Christian guidance.

The Bible tells us what God commands as well as how he commands. The Spirit of Jesus can be expected to lead the Christian in definite directions. Discipleship is not an open-ended call to radical obedience. We can expect the call to specify directions that the grateful correspondence of faith will prefer: indifference toward possessions and worldly honors, renunciation of force, dissolution of familial attachments, freedom from self-justifying religion and the overriding directive to take up the cross.[39]

Finally, one must admit that something is missing from this theological ethics. All the characteristics of the moral agent are derived from the event of being addressed by the Word of God. Moral agents have character, a unique history and moral responsibility only because they are constantly addressed by God. The self cannot be considered apart from God's action. This leads to an impoverished view of moral experience because there seems to be no self between moments when God is commanding. Moral life is more than simply discrete moments of decision; it refers to the continuous aspects of the self: virtues and vices, character, identity, memory, commitments and roles. Even if one grants the priority of the faith assent over moral reflection on theological grounds, Barth seems to have maximized the role of obedient faith at the expense of a coherent sense of the moral self.

Even though Barth restored both the normative and dispositional resources to Christian ethics that his existentialist colleagues wanted to banish, the moral life remains a sporadic affair. Besides the model of call and response, we must pay attention to additional biblical material to redress this existentialist imbalance. The next chapter will show how the continuous features of human existence —nature, reason, role-obligations—ground a very different Christian ethics of natural law that also finds support in the pluralism of Scripture.

# 2
# Scripture as Moral Reminder

Our second approach to the use of Scripture in ethics stresses moral norms but not in the fashion of Barth and Bonhoeffer. For them moral directives were immediately communicated to the individual by the commanding God whereas in this approach we will see a morality embedded in humanity through God's creative work. The moral question here receives a humanistic answer even if that humanism has a theological bent. This approach's answer to the question "What ought I to do?" is simply, "Be human, for the Lord has redemptively accepted your humanity in the incarnation." God's intentions for humanity are structured into our innermost drives and recognized by reasonable reflection. The grace of Christ restores and elevates that humanity which never completely lost its status as "image of God." When we recognize what is authentically human, we are in effect discovering the will of God for us. Scripture *reminds* us what it means to be human and calls us to live an integral human life that our egotism would ignore. However, the Gospel does not ask us to be something other than human; rather it calls us to full humanity in relation to God and empowers us to live it. Christians believe that full humanity is possible only through the grace of Christ.

This approach begins from ethics, the theory of what is normatively human, and that controls its use of the other sources of Christian ethics: Scripture, tradition and pertinent empirical data. We saw that Barth's ethics was primarily theological because he used the central doctrines of election, reconciliation, and sanctification to interpret the other sources. A weak existentialist ethics permitted him to discount the role of general moral principles. We will see the opposite approach in this chapter. The strong suit of moral theology in the Roman Catholic tradition has been natural law; only recently has it turned to Scripture for a more theological vision of the moral agent.

In the course of this book, we will examine a number of positions that are theologically rich but weak in presenting practical procedures to answer specific moral questions. Those who use Scripture as moral reminder face the opposite challenge. The finely tuned practicality of natural law ethics can judge what is morally right with scarcely any reference to Christ or the theological beliefs that guide Christian life. Because natural law ethics attempts to settle moral questions on the basis of the humanity that believers have in common with non-believers, it tries to speak in natural, human terms rather than theological language. This can provide a reality test on religious inspirations to action: Do they measure up to ordinary human morality? By bracketing Christian convictions, however, natural law ethics can lead to a denigration of a distinctively Christian faith vision. This certainly happened with some of the older moral theologians whose moral casuistry seemed to operate in a theological vacuum, untouched by any reference to Christ, the role of the Spirit, sanctification, or discipleship.

Since 1950, Roman Catholic moral theology has been undergoing an historic transformation as religious experience and biblical material have been integrated into its procedures. We will examine two periods of the writings of Josef Fuchs, the key figure in this transformation. Fuchs is a German Jesuit who has taught for many years at the Gregorian University in Rome. (He suggested to the author that this chapter be entitled "Scripture as Moral Reminder" rather than "Moral Teacher.") Prior to the Second Vatican Council, Fuchs responded to neo-Orthodox criticism of moral theology by demonstrating a biblical foundation for natural law. Since the Council he has developed a more Christocentric moral theology by incorporating the insights of Karl Rahner, the foremost Catholic theologian of this century. We will also consider Bruno Schüller, a German moral theologian who has also contributed to this renewal of moral theology. Because this approach begins with natural law, let us first sketch this system and then examine Fuchs' earlier efforts to articulate its theological and biblical foundations.

## I. Natural Law

The noted Anglican theologian John Macquarrie writes that "natural law is foundational to morality. It is the inner drive toward authentic personhood and is presupposed in all particular ethical traditions, including the Christian one."[1] How else can we discover what is right and wrong, good or evil, except by measuring actions against our humanity? Every ethics presumes that the author and the readers share a common humanity which gives them some capacity to infer what is right from that common humanity. Morality is based on humanity because whatever is right and good is consistent with humanity. Natural law is foundational in the sense that it is objective rather than arbitrary. Morality is not established by social convention or by legislation of the powerful. It is objective because it rests on a given—"the inner drive toward authentic personhood."

For example, according to natural law theory lying is not immoral because we have a commandment from the Old Testament that forbids it. Lying is wrong because it violates our humanity; it is unnatural and inhuman. It destroys trustworthy human communication, which is indispensable for living in community. Without community we would perish, or at least be severely crippled. The divine commandment against lying reminds us that lying destroys our humanity. The command is there because lying is wrong; lying is not wrong simply because a commandment forbids it.

Natural law simply means that our own human nature functions as a kind of basic "law" because it regulates our conduct. Natural law is not a code of regulations to consult when solving moral quandaries. It is a process of reflection rather than the codified results of such reflection. Natural law thinking has taken many forms since its first articulation among the Greeks. Although medieval theology produced some relatively conservative forms of natural law thinking, such thought has been revolutionary at other times, as when it grounded the call for human rights during the French Revolution.[2] The persistent challenge is to determine which practices are truly natural and which are so fixed in culture that they are taken to be "natural." Despite the fact that enslavement of some races and the subjugation of women were long held to be natural practices, their abolition came in large part from a natural law argument: to deny these groups civil and economic rights is to deny their human dignity.

## Thomas Aquinas on Natural Morality

What has given natural law theologians confidence in human reason and its ability to determine what is humanly right is the doctrine of creation. In the *Summa Theologiae,* Thomas Aquinas grounds the natural law in the "eternal law" that is the paradigm in God's intellect for every creature.[3] In most of creation, this paradigm is patterned into creatures only through their instincts; their natural behavior is instinctually determined. Human beings have certain drives too, but they also have the reflective capacity of reason and a degree of choice about their conduct. Within the "given" of certain natural drives and necessities, we have to determine what will lead to our human flourishing and choose to act humanly. The basic drives for survival, procreation and family, seeking the truth and living in community are the given points of departure of moral reflection. Our reflection begins from these drives to determine what is humanly right in a given situation. We are neither programmed for automatic development, nor open to every possible pattern of behavior. Certain forms of behavior are self-defeating because they violate our humanity.

Every person in every culture desires happiness—human flourishing—but no one knows exactly what happiness is. Human reason reflects on and tries to reconcile the basic drives and the necessities for living together to discern the appropriate practical action. Reason must also be guided by sound inclinations or virtues in order to be consistent and accurate in its reflection and in its behavior. Courage, prudence, justice and temperance are all necessary to perceive the courageous, prudent, and fair course of action. Virtues humanize our basic drives. For example, it takes not only intelligence but virtue to develop policies of national survival when we are faced with the ominous possibility of nuclear holocaust. Although natural law does not guarantee unanimity on such intricate questions, it does provide a common starting point for the debate that is rooted in the humanity of all participants. Aquinas relied more on the guidance of virtue than the deductive capacities of reason in deciding what was normatively human.

The *Summa Theologiae* does not indicate a radical transformation of humanity through the redemptive action of Christ. It is primarily a theology of creation and restoration. As the argument unfolds the theory of human capacities, the quest for happiness and the virtues are all determined with almost no reference to Christ. Even after the Fall, God's creative pattern still persists in human beings since even a damaged intellect and will image the Creator to some degree. Aquinas brings in the person of Christ only in the third and final part of the *Summa,* when he argues that Christ restores humanity and leads it back to the Creator. The grace of Christ justifies human beings and elevates their moral virtues by charity, which is a share in the divine life.

We do not find in the plan or the language of the *Summa* the metaphors of radical transformation that characterize parts of the New Testament, especially in John and Paul. Fallen human nature is redeemed by God's grace but this restoration is not described as a radical transition from death to life, from darkness to light or from bondage to freedom. Aquinas describes a restored humanity rather than a completely new creation. The impact of Christ's grace on morality follows this same pattern. Fallen humanity had to know what was right or it would not have been capable of sin. The effects of the Fall were felt mostly in the will by an inability to desire and choose what was right. According to Aquinas, the new "law of Christ" is primarily the gift of the Holy Spirit, which enables the moral agent to desire what is good and accomplish it with ease and delight. The written law is secondary and it does not impose any obligations that were not always part of natural law.[4] Our vocation to be Christian converges with our vocation to be human.

Because charity and the virtues were central to his ethics, Aquinas' version of natural law focused on the moral *agent* rather than on individual moral *acts.* The moral theology that followed the Council of Trent reversed this focus. The textbooks of moral theology presumed and largely ignored the theological framework of Christian life and concentrated on solving moral questions about particular actions. The ecclesiastical function of moral theology shaped its method. Priests had to be trained to hear sacramental confessions and assist their penitents in recognizing their sins. They also had to prevent people from finding sin where there was none. Law, rather than Gospel, shaped this moral theology as it trained priests to be judges of moral acts and provide absolution for specific sins that were confessed. Moral theology allied itself with the discipline of canon law rather than with "ascetical" and "mystical theology," which dealt with Christian growth and sanctification. Bernard Häring, Josef Fuchs and a whole generation of Catholic moralists have tried to redress this imbalance.[5] In doing so, they have not ignored the moral act but have developed a richly theological vision of the moral agent.

Moral theology still strives to develop careful procedures that allow movement from rational moral principles to particular cases. It still articulates moral questions in a "public" language that is meant to be understood by any person of good will. But a shift in moral theology is becoming apparent, even in the official social encyclicals of the Catholic Church. From the time of Leo XIII more than a century ago to *Pacem in Terris* of John XXIII in 1962, these papal teachings were couched in the philosophical language of natural law. They did not use biblical doctrines or symbols to argue for the rights of labor, the responsibilities of private property, the just claims of immigrants and the poor, or the human rights that no government could justly deny. The documents of Vatican II and the subsequent social encyclicals used more biblical material and made a more distinct religious appeal. But integrating biblical perspectives with the public language is difficult, as evidenced by the recent efforts of the American Catholic bishops to articulate a pastoral response to the nuclear crisis. The juxtaposition of biblical theology of peace and secular analysis of just war precludes integration.[6]

## II.  Josef Fuchs: A Biblical Natural Law

In *Natural Law: A Theological Investigation,* Fuchs clarified the theological foundations of natural law in response to the charges of Barth and Emil Brunner that it was unbiblical and divorced from the saving work of Christ.[7] Although Fuchs' work during and after the Vatican Council (1962–66) incorporates the thought of Rahner and has a more Christocentric view of the moral agent, this earlier book stands as a classic defense of natural law incorporating biblical material.

Before developing a Christological argument from a variety of New Testament sources, Fuchs begins with the passage that traditionally has justified natural law, the first two chapters of Romans. In Romans 1—3, Paul demonstrates the universal culpability of Jew and Gentile and the corresponding universal need for Christ. The people of Israel were accountable for their sins because they had the Law even though they did not observe it. What about the Gentiles? Paul argues that they, too, were culpable because they knew what was right from the law that was part of their own nature. The Mosaic Law did not declare anything right or wrong but simply clarified for Israel what was naturally moral. Fuchs writes, "Since the Law does not *establish* the difference between good and evil but rather teaches men about what is already good or evil, St. Paul can say that the good works of the heathen constitute a fulfilment of the demands of the Law. 'They do what the Law requires' (Rom 2:14) and they do it 'by nature' (Rom 2:14 vide 27). Although they do not have the Law of Moses (Rom 2:14) nonetheless 'what the Law requires is written in their hearts' (Rom 2:15) so that 'they are a law unto themselves' (Rom 2:14). 'Their consciences and their thoughts, accusing or perhaps excusing them, bear witness to that' (Rom 2:15)."[8] If the Gentiles were morally accountable, too, then morality did not depend on the positive revelation in the Bible. Presumably, the Jews also had this inner law that the Mosaic Law reminded them to follow.

If the Fall had totally eradicated any notion of morality from human beings, then the argument of Romans 1 and 2 would not hold. It is impossible to hold someone morally accountable who is totally depraved and lacks any knowledge of what is right and good. Human intellect and will, the capacities that make humanity the image of God, are weakened morally in such a person, but never destroyed. Fuchs notes that Protestant thought has a different notion of being "in the image of God." For Protestants, he writes, the "likeness to God consists only in responsibility and in the fact of being called and in responding. That is to say that Protestant thought finds our likeness to God in a relation."[9] When that relation is broken, the likeness to God disappears until it is restored by God in Christ. Catholic theology, by contrast, holds for a humanity that images God even after the Fall and that cannot be eradicated by sin. Humans image God in their reason and freedom; therefore, even sinners have not lost God's image completely.

Failure to respond to the God who can be known from creation leads to moral depravity as is testified in Romans 1:18–32, Galatians 4:15, 1 Thessalonians 4—5 and 1 Corinthians 1:21. Fuchs writes, "The moral order violated in this way was, for St. Paul, equivalent to that called natural law by the church now."[10]

Creation is not a theologically insignificant basis for Christian ethics because the New Testament teaches that creation was from the beginning oriented to the incarnation of the Word. Fuchs notes that "Scripture in fact tells us that in him and for him all things were created (cf. Col 1:15–17; Eph 1:9–23; 1 Cor 8:6.)[11] . . . In the God-man the Father has given us the prototype of the Christian. . . . He is our prototype because he is truly man and realizes in himself the essence of man's natural being, no more and no less than we do."[12] Once again, the Christology of a theological system fits the ethical model it contains. The Son of God has redemptively embraced our humanity in the incarnation, and that humanity was originally created with just this union in view. Therefore, we can be confident of some continuity between human nature and the grace of Christ; the redemption will not bring about a totally distinct creation. Christ empowers us to a life that surpasses mere fulfillment of the natural law without setting aside that inner law of our humanity. The natural law is not in itself salvific even if it can instruct us in what conduct will, with grace, be salvific.

Jesus Christ shows in himself what true humanity is meant to be, and he empowers the Christian to live this full humanity. In the Gospels Jesus does not impose any new moral burdens but merely brings to light what was already naturally binding. Some of his demands may seem to exceed what is naturally reasonable, but only because we are limited by the egotism of sin. For example, the indissolubility of marriage is what God intended from the beginning. When Jesus condemns Jewish divorce practices in Matthew 19, he does not cite himself as the authority but refers back to God's original intention that "the two shall become one flesh" (Gen 2:24). Fuchs comments, "The law of the indissolubility of marriage is proved not only in general by reference to the will of God but more precisely by reference to the will of God expressed in the nature of the created human being."[13] For Barth, the permanence of marriage derived from the call to mirror forth the covenant fidelity of God; for the natural law tradition, the objective human reality of marriage demands its permanence.

God can call individuals to unique vocations through the action of the Holy Spirit, but Fuchs does not believe that vocational experiences are the paradigm of Christian morality. God's will is ordinarily mediated through the human experience of the Christian. Indeed, we should see a true, if mediated, response to God in the ordinary duties of our lives. "Moreover," asserts Fuchs, "to emphasize this explicitly it is of vital importance from the moral and religious point of view that we conceive the demand of the natural law in the concrete situation as the personal demand of God to the personal man. The spiritual encounter of man with his own being, the confrontation of his interior and exterior worlds, is in fact an encounter with God."[14] To preserve God's sovereignty, Barth at times emphasized the discontinuities between ordinary human morality and the command of God. Fuchs, on the other hand, stresses the continuity to safeguard the consistency between God and his creation. For both theologians, however, the absoluteness of the moral demand ultimately rests on the authority of the Absolute God.

We can never find "nature" in a condition that is totally unaffected by the grace of God. Every person is constantly being called by God, even if he or she refuses the invitations. No one can know—or meet—the demands of morality without the presence of grace, even if the recipient of the summons does not acknowledge it as grace. Fuchs develops a complex notion of a human nature that is always touched by the "supernatural," the divine reality. This argument provides a better explanation than most other theologies of how some religiously indifferent people can live moral lives. In striving to do what is right, they are being supported by the grace of God and are "anonymously" responding to God's reality.

## III. Human Values and Christian Morality: Karl Rahner

Most of the development in moral theology since Vatican II has been in the area of the moral agent rather than the moral act. Scripture plays a larger role in describing the transformation of the agent's motives under the influence of Christ and the Spirit. In regard to specific acts, more attention is paid to consequences as determinative of morality than to application of universal principles to cases. Fuchs and other moralists insist that Scripture does not offer much new information about what acts are right and wrong; such knowledge is already established by our humanity.

Fuchs was one of the chief architects of the Council's call for more biblical and Christocentric moral theology, for a return to the sources of religious experience.[15] He has since used the model of human experience taught by Karl Rahner to adapt the natural law tradition from within. The result has been a two-layered approach to Christian morality that connects the inner law of Christian love to natural law. Hence a book of his post-conciliar writings is entitled *Human Values and Christian Morality.*[16] "Christian morality" is agent-centered because it is that life lived by people who have surrendered themselves to God in Christ. They express that commitment in "human values" that are identical in content with sound natural morality.

Fuchs finds in Paul, Thomas Aquinas and Karl Rahner this basic distinction between Christian moral agency and natural moral standards. Paul presumes that there are many standard vices which should be repugnant to Christians and to everyone else (1 Cor 6:9–10; Gal 5:19–21; Rom 1:29–31). When discussing the immorality of fornication with prostitutes in 1 Corinthians 6:12–20, he takes it for granted that the readers understand that it is morally wrong. He provides new motivation for avoiding such a practice by citing eschatological and ecclesial reasons. "According to Paul," writes Fuchs, "the same material norm of moral living, a truly human norm, applies objectively to Christians and non-Christians, Jews and Gentiles (cf. Rom 2:1f, 6–11). . . . Christians too, Jews and Gentiles, can discern what is honorable and dishonorable, moral and immoral."[17] Paul only occasionally recommends specific conduct whereas he dwells at length on the new attitudes, perspectives and convictions that the Christian should have in Christ.

Thomas Aquinas reflects this two-layered approach in his statement that the law of Christ is primarily the gift of the Holy Spirit that animates the moral agent and secondarily the written letter of moral norms and principles. Too many followers of Aquinas read his treatise on law in the *Summa* without reading the treatise on grace which follows it.[18] The subsequent section on the virtues explains how transformed moral agency is the basis of moral choice. The virtuous person has a "connatural knowledge" of the appropriate action. The just person will often spontaneously have a sense of the fair thing to do without having to reason about the rules of justice. Charity introduces a type of Christian connaturality into the virtues. These capacities of the agent were often overlooked by the moralists who confined themselves to the rational model of the law treatise.

## *Karl Rahner: A New Foundation for Moral Theology*

Karl Rahner provides the theoretical foundation for the relation of the inner law of Christian love to the particular acts that love is expressed in. He distinguishes between the basic act of freedom in which the person commits himself or herself to God, and the individual acts of free choice that constitute the moral life. The basic self-surrender to God is a "transcendental act" because it defines the person as a whole in relation to the gift of God's life and love. This surrender, however, is not a single decision made at one moment, but the summation and unity of the individual's history. The basic orientation toward God or away from God is constituted by particular "categorical acts" of daily life. These form the material of radical commitment, and common affirmations of the good that shape a life that says yes to God rather than no.

In John 14, Jesus speaks both of his disciples' love for him (that radical self-commitment) and the commandments necessarily connected with it. Fuchs writes of this distinction:

> It is not a specific act of love but the transcendental love acting out of basic freedom that necessarily lives and expresses itself in the keeping of his word through the various acts of free choice. This difference between the person as a

whole, whom we have at our disposal in basic freedom, and the person's acts, which we determine by free choice, is also meant when Scripture says that God looks not only at a man's deeds but also at his heart, that the Holy Spirit by grace gives a new heart; and this is the sense wherever the biblical speech of the Old and New Testament uses the concept of the heart to signify the depths of the human person.[19]

The heart refers to the agent in the deepest, most personal level. It is this innermost level that will be transformed by the gift of the Spirit, not only the individual acts of obedience.

When the Christian is given this new heart, he or she adopts a whole new posture toward others and toward God, a stance that Fuchs calls "Christian intentionality." It transforms natural obligations and virtues from within by giving them a personal reference to God they could not have on their own. Moreover, the power of the Spirit makes these obligations and virtues part of the person's character so they become habitual. In content, these virtues and moral standards are what constitute any serious moral life. God's will is unitary: that we be human in Christ. For example, Christians will act justly both in response to the same standards any just person will follow, and out of love of God inspired by their Christian intentionality. "Christian motivation," Fuchs states, "provides human conduct with a deeper and richer meaning, which is subjectively part of the action itself."[20] Objectively, the "categorical" standards of justice, honesty, and the like are no different from the natural law that binds everyone.

By adopting Rahner's position, Fuchs has introduced a new definition of human nature into natural law. Does this lead to a different kind of morality than that stemming from the more traditional notion of nature proposed by Aquinas? I believe it does. For Rahner, the person is at the core "self-defining freedom" before the mystery which is God.[21] Although this is not incompatible with human nature as described by Aristotle and Aquinas, it is clearly more open-ended. A more optimistic attitude toward human development and self-definition emerges because the moral life is a task more of freedom than of observing the known limits of human nature. In a more recent work, Fuchs writes, "If we wish to speak of God's will, this is nothing else than the divine desire that man might exist and live. This implies, however, that he live as man, that he discover himself and his world as well as their latent possibilities, that he understand them, that he shape and realize himself as genuinely human, as bodily-spiritual being."[22] Fuchs' shift in practical method is consistent with this, as he has carefully moved away from an older notion of absolute moral principles to a greater reliance on consequences.

This new notion of human nature will affect the way Scripture is used in ethics. Passages expressing the transformation of the agent will obviously be more welcome than those dwelling on specific patterns of conduct. Fuchs does write of the imitation of Christ but less specifically than the proponents of a discipleship approach to the Gospel. Both Rahner and Fuchs seem more open to the specific discernment of vocation by the individual than to the specific mandates of the New Testament. It may be that Rahner's reluctance to write about ethics results from a weakness in his model of human experience. When self-defining freedom is the core of humanity, it may be difficult to derive any moral principles except in a very formal way. (For example, immoral actions would be those that contradict transcendental freedom.)[23] Certain moral demands appear to be made on the disciples of Christ in the New Testament that are not easily reconcilable with human prudence: a preference for the outcast, costly service even unto death, taking others' needs more seriously than your own. How are these categorical actions connected with transcendental freedom? Are there Christian ways of acting as well as Christian intentionality?

## A Distinctive Christian Ethics?

Twentieth century theologians have often proposed that there is a distinctive content to the ethics in Scripture, and they have indicated as evidence those passages that seem to surpass what would normally be expected in philosophical morality. The hard sayings of the Gospel do appear to have a heroic character that is above and beyond the call of duty: love your enemies, take up the cross daily, turn the other cheek, love without thought of return. Would these seem reasonable to a good person who was not guided by allegiance to Jesus of Nazareth and moved by his Spirit?

Fuchs analyzes each of these passages in order to sustain his thesis that Scripture adds no new obligations beyond the natural law. Is it already a human obligation to help those from whom we expect no recompense? Is it naturally obligatory to love our enemies? His answer is revealing: "To this it can be answered—were that so, then those who do not know or acknowledge Christ would be permitted to leave unregarded their neighbour, the sick, the needy, the under-developed countries, indeed they would be permitted to hate their enemies and, consequently, to practise the method of hatred, violence, and so on."[24] The core of every genuine human morality is love of neighbor, whether that neighbor be estranged from us or not.

We next turn to the command to take up the cross and follow Jesus, the paradigmatic moment for Bonhoeffer. Does every natural morality contain the cost of discipleship? Fuchs argues that every serious moral existence involves a considerable degree of renunciation, which forces the agent to a self-transcendence that is liable to be costly. Non-Christians and atheists "too experience their egoism as 'fallen' men and are able to understand that in this situation renunciation and self-denial, hence the cross, may be part of authentic being-human."[25] However, only those who know the full story of fallen humanity and the redemption that comes through the cross and resurrection of Jesus Christ can comprehend the full depth of the Christian doctrine of the cross.

Fuchs warns against making comparisons of this sort merely rhetorical by comparing natural morality at its worst with Christian morality at its best. Rather, we should compare the best instances of each to determine if there is more common ground than we first expected. I am still not convinced, however, that the command to bear the cross can be abstracted from the personal story of Jesus of Nazareth. Jesus did not only say, "Take up your cross daily," but immediately added "and follow me." As Bonhoeffer said, Jesus stands between the disciple and the costly demand, thereby altering its meaning significantly.

The Sermon on the Mount offers the strongest challenge to those who assert an identity of content between natural and human morality on the categorical level. It seems to call us to heroic acts of indiscriminate love, non-violence, purity of heart, and forgiveness that would be unthinkable apart from the Kingdom of God. The pacifist and monastic traditions in Christianity have interpreted these demands as the New Law of Christ, personal commands to be obeyed to the letter. Fuchs takes a different tack, "The true meaning of its individual demands must be drawn not from the literal text, but from interpreting hyperbolic ways of speaking; then they will be understood not as legal obligations, but rather as daring 'ethical models.' " The Sermon on the Mount does not reject humanity as such, but just fallen, egotistical humanity. If the Sermon's demands grate on our sensibilities, it is because we ourselves remain unconverted. "Insofar as we renounce our egoism in grace, we will understand the demands of the Sermon on the Mount—which are the demands of love—not as negating our being-human, but as its purest expression."[26] Even when there are demands which are specific to the Christian community, such as a call to virginity or to worship in specific ways, these are simply expressions of duties inherent in the natural law. If we believe that humanity is fully revealed only in the One in whom it was created, there can be only one basic imperative for Christian morality: "Be human."

### IV.  Bruno Schüller: Biblical Exhortation Not Instruction

Bruno Schüller agrees that on the categorical level there can be no distinctive Christian ethics. Some of the exhortatory or "paranetic" passages of Scripture appear to give new meaning to certain moral duties by linking them to the story of salvation in Yahweh and Jesus. Theologians express this link by saying that in biblical morality the *imperative* is based on the *indicative* of what God has done for us. Schüller distinguishes the ethical "truth-value" of these passages from their "effect-value." To a great extent, biblical ethics is exhortatory. But one must concede, Schüller insists, that "exhortation of itself does not convey any new moral insights."[27] On the contrary, exhortation presumes that the audience knows what to do but needs to be encouraged to actually do it. Jesus may supply the motive for Christian morality, but he does not supply the standard. This is true even when Christians are urged to treat others as God has treated them, as in the new commandment of Jesus in John 15:12, "This is my commandment, that you love one another as I have loved you."

For Schüller, the relationship between Law and Gospel is fundamentally another example of the ordinary norm of morality, the golden rule. Scriptural passages that call readers to "imitation of Christ" exemplify the golden rule, which mandates us to "treat others as you wish others to treat you." By recalling the good others have done for us (including God and Christ), we derive our standards for doing good to others. Schüller concludes, "Then the relationship between gospel and law (covenant and torah) seems to be simply the golden rule as reexpressed in the first of our . . . formulations: God has done good to you; you should likewise do good to others."[28] At all costs, Schüller wants to avoid a "Christonomous moral positivism" which he finds in Barth and others, whereby mercy or justice is good only because Christ has decreed it so. Christian motivations may deepen the subjective meaning of justice and compassion, but they cannot constitute their moral validity.

This confidence in the golden rule as the norm of morality may indicate a different anthropology operating in Schüller's ethics from that in Fuchs'. Schüller's position seems to be Kantian rather than Rahnerian in its overtones of the categorical imperative, where logical self-consistency is the basis for the moral norm. I will argue in a later chapter that the central dynamic of biblical ethics is responding love and that Schüller's position does not do full justice to that response because it too readily prescinds from the historical revelation of the One we are responding to in faith.

When Scripture is a moral reminder, the theologian is less bound by some of its particular mandates, which we now see are limits of an outdated culture. The more flexible notion of human nature in more recent moral theology admits that nature does change through history. Hence, some of the institutions that were taken for granted as natural in the Mediterranean cultures of the first century are no longer binding for us today. Just as human nature changes with time, so do the moral standards flowing from it.

Schüller asks, "What of the NT admonition that wives be subject to their husbands in all things? This obviously presupposes a lack of 'age' on the wife's part no longer valid—at least for most of the Western world. Today the model for the relation of husband and wife is rather one of equal partners with no one-sided superiority or subjection." This flexibility may seem to raise the specter of cultural relativism in which all values are relative only to particular cultures and are inapplicable outside them. Not necessarily, replies Schüller, "for the husband/wife relationship has objectively changed and with it the ethical precepts appropriate for them."[29] More general attitudes based on the Gospel will have permanent relevance because they are necessary ingredients of the transformation of the moral agent. However, the standards for particular moral acts will change as human nature and institutions change. "Absolutes" will be found on the level of values and attitudes rather than in unvarying moral norms that are applicable without exception.

### Problems in the Revision?

Moral theology in this vein has applied biblical material to the moral agent but in principle has been reluctant to apply it to moral acts. I believe this is due in part to a continuing commitment to express practical ethics in a language that is understandable to all reasonable people, which would seem to rule out specific biblical norms or symbols. At a deeper level, the model of human experience that moral theology has borrowed from Rahner may be deficient in dealing with the moral act itself. Rahner locates the impact of grace on the transcendental level of basic freedom rather than on the categorical level of concrete choices, except where there is a personal invitation from God meant only for the individual Christian. God's revelation, however, took place in a very categorical fashion, in a particular person who had a particular way of dealing with others. That revelation may indicate more than a basic disposition to love the neighbor; it may also command us to love the neighbor in a specific way that is derived from the story of Jesus in the Gospel.

Under the umbrella of Rahner's theory of human experience one finds a wide variety of practical approaches to categorical moral questions. Some are more consequentialist, others more Kantian, others more intuitionist in their handling of particular cases. In part, the sophistication of Catholic moral casuistry has been aided by a greater confidence than most Protestants would have that Law is a necessary dimension of Gospel. However, I believe that the current sophisticated approaches to practical moral reasoning show the same resistance to biblical material that the older Scholastic moralists did. Ironically, this most practical of the schools of Christian ethics pays the least attention to the actual moral norms found in the Bible. Nevertheless, the restoration of biblical teaching on the transformation of the agent's heart is a major improvement over the older moral theology.

In the following chapters we will continue to see a concentration on biblical teachings regarding the agent rather than on the moral act. A closer link will be drawn to connect the act to the dispositions and perspectives of the Christian agent. In the fourth chapter H. Richard Niebuhr proposes a form of intuitive discerning vision that uses biblical symbols to illuminate what God is doing in specific situations and indicate a fitting response. Stanley Hauerwas then argues that the character of the Christian agent must be governed by the story of Jesus present in the Gospels and lived out through distinctive intentions and attitudes evolving from that story. In the final chapter I will argue that "Christian affections" are the link between character and action that is consonant with Gospel values. Liberation theology requires willingness to aid the poor and oppressed as a necessary prerequisite for doing Christian theology or ethics. All of these views are attempts to bridge the gap between the transcendental level of "Christian intentionality" and the categorical level of particular acts.

Although these alternative theories integrate passages from Scripture that depend on the distinctive events and qualities revealed in Yahweh and Jesus, they tend to neglect other forms of biblical morality. Wisdom literature, the common sense appeals of the parables, practical moral instruction based on the consistent lessons of creation rather than the revelatory events of salvation history—all of this material is best accommodated to Christian ethics by those who use Scripture as moral reminder. For the Bible's more novel moral dimensions we must turn to other approaches and to other literary genres within the canon.

# 3
# Call to Liberation

During the past decade, a new use of Scripture has emerged in the theologies of liberation. It first appeared among Latin American theologians and was then adapted by first world feminists to address their own situation in a male-dominated culture. It answers the moral question "What ought I to do?" with the most specific moral imperative we have yet seen: "Act to liberate the oppressed because God is on their side." This imperative is the result of reading Scripture in a particular context of historical and social analysis as liberationists search for a "usable past" to guide their commitment to social transformation today. It is not the immediate command of God, nor simply the discernment of where God is acting in history; in some ways, more than any other approach, it is more akin to using Scripture as moral reminder.

How can this view avoid exploiting the Bible as simply a rhetorical support for political strategies that have actually been derived from purely secular sources? The use of Scripture as call to liberation shares this danger with all our previous models. No one is immune from the "hermeneutical circle," from "discovering" in Scripture interests that were established prior to interpreting the Word of God. Every use of Scripture begins from some interest, but does that use allow Scripture to challenge that original position? The initial interest, such as preference for the poor, may have originated in a biblically informed set of values, and may then be brought to Scripture for deepening or modification. Every use of Scripture has to show that the Word of God can still be a "two-edged sword" that can shape its presuppositions. Otherwise, the Word will only be used decoratively for a pre-established moral preference.

The charter document for liberation theology is Gustavo Gutierrez' *A Theology of Liberation*.[1] He is straightforward in his theoretical foundations, even if some subsequent liberation theologies have been criticized as spiritualities in search of a theological foundation. His theology is based on an analysis of the historical and economic situation of Latin America and a utopian vision of possible new forms of humanity. From this theoretical base he selects and interprets mainly Old Testament historical accounts and prophetic material, concentrating on the symbol of the exodus. We will also briefly examine two feminist approaches to Scripture. Letty M. Russell's *Human Liberation in a Feminist Perspective* consciously applies Gutierrez' method to the situation of woman in American culture, particularly in the churches.[2] She reworks biblical texts that have previously been given a patriarchal interpretation and advances the biblical notion of servanthood as basis for new forms of partnership between men and women. Phyllis Trible's *God and the Rhetoric of Sexuality* is an excellent literary analysis of three Old Testament passages with applications that illuminate human sexuality as imaging God's reality.[3]

## I. Gustavo Gutierrez: Commitment to the Oppressed

No neutral reading of Scripture can discern the call to liberation; such a call presupposes a commitment to the poor and oppressed and a willingness to act on their behalf. Niebuhr wrote that revelation is unintelligible from the spectator's viewpoint. Gutierrez goes one step further, insisting that only someone participating in the struggle for justice can hear God's Word. All reflection arises out of praxis, out of committed action on behalf of some cause. The neutral observer is already committed to maintain the status quo even if he or she does not admit it. "First comes the commitment to charity, to service," writes Gutierrez. "Theology comes 'later.' It is second. The Church's pastoral action is not arrived at as a conclusion from theological premises. Theology does not lead to pastoral activity, but is rather reflection on it."[4]

Faith is the understanding of a commitment, a definite attitude toward God and neighbor that is assumed in light of the revealed Word of God. Because love is the center of Christian life, a non-committal faith is a contradiction. Theology that reflects upon commitment must be a liberating theology because it moves from reflection on the world to taking part in the transformation of the world. Revelation demands commitment to the poor and needy as integral to true religion; genuine theology, therefore, must arise from such commitment and action. Identification with the poor is the privileged standpoint that discloses the meaning of Scripture: "In this participation [in the process of liberation]," writes Gutierrez, "will be heard nuances of the Word of God which are imperceptible in other existential situations and without which there can be no authentic and fruitful faithfulness to the Lord."[5] Pastoral practice will be challenged by the Word in turn, but only engagement in the work of social transformation will expose the true meaning of the text.

Avery Dulles, S.J. noted this as a significant new definition of faith for Christians. When faith is conceived as assent to authoritatively revealed truths, its goal is illumination. Aquinas and Augustine have been used to support this traditional notion of faith. When Luther redefined faith as surrender in confidence to God's gracious gift in Christ, faith shifted to a fiducial meaning, an act of radical personal trust in God. At times the emphasis on justification by faith alone obscured the sense of human responsibility in the political arena and led to moral passivity, which Bonhoeffer attacked. Liberation theology calls for a third form of faith assent which Dulles describes as "performative."[6] Moral commitment is added to intellectual conviction and personal trust because the acting out of truth is necessary for the belief in it. If I am on the side of the privileged, how can I ever discover that the God of revelation is found on the side of the oppressed? This latter conviction must be proved by sound textual study, but the right disposition must be brought to that study. (At times, liberation theology may present this as a self-evident truth; others may respond that God is on no one's side, but on everyone's as he acts in judgment, creation and redemption.)

Scripture is only one source of this critical commitment to liberation. We mentioned earlier that every adequate Christian ethics has four components: Scripture, tradition, a theory of what is normatively human (ethics), and empirical data relevant to the issues considered. Liberation theology, especially as presented by Gutierrez, emphasizes the latter two components. One should note the similarities to traditional Catholic moral theology, at least as far as method goes. A theory of human existence and careful factual analysis control all reference to Scripture and tradition. For moral theology, the theory of what is normatively human is natural law, while for liberation theology it is a specific form of historical and social analysis. The very structure of Gutierrez' book demonstrates this priority of social analysis. We come to the biblical material only in the fourth and final section of the argument after lengthy presentations of Latin American economic and political structures and the Catholic Church's reaction to them. The second normative element is a socialist "utopian" vision of a new unoppressed humanity, which also guides the interpretation of Scripture. This theology does not pretend to give a timeless and universal reading of Scripture; it argues from its specific social location, "the view from below."

Readers familiar with Marx will recognize his influence on Gutierrez' analysis of social structures, but Gutierrez is not a doctrinaire Marxist; Marxism is simply the most pertinent theory for the Latin American scene. Class struggle is so obvious in the third world that there is no sense in pretending it does not exist. Gutierrez also accepts the position that the values of individuals are formed by the economic structures they are confined to. Accordingly, Christian conversion involves both a repudiation of the exploiting structures of society and a willingness to transform them into more humane systems so that people living under them can become more human. "Our conversion process is affected by the socio-economic, political, cultural, and human environment in which it occurs," writes Gutierrez. "Without a change in these structures, there is no authentic conversion."[7] No private, spiritualized conversion is adequate for this performative notion of faith any more than it was adequate for the Letter of James, which demands that good works authenticate Christian faith.

## Liberation and Exodus

Exodus is the paradigm for the action of God in history, especially as interpreted through the prophets and the theology of Deutero-Isaiah. Three themes of the Old Testament define the meaning of exodus for Gutierrez: the link between salvation and creation, the eschatological promises of the prophets and the closeness of God to Israel as Emmanuel. Each of these finds its fulfillment in Jesus Christ, but he does not radically alter them. After examining these three interrelated themes, we will analyze the relation between the Kingdom of God and human political efforts.

The exodus symbol becomes a "root metaphor" for liberationists but it functions differently from symbols in H. Richard Niebuhr. It is more an historical instance to which God's people can refer than a lens through which they might read the signs of the times. Exodus is a concrete event of human liberation that can motivate believers today in their struggle against oppression. Gutierrez does not indicate that God is acting in history except through human effort. "The word liberation," he writes, "allows for another approach to the biblical sources which inspire the presence and action of man in history."[8] Discernment of appropriate action comes out of social and economic analysis rather than from Niebuhr's search for an appropriate response to the present action of God. Exodus points out the conflictual character of class struggle in the so-called underdeveloped nations and indicates that the core of Christian existence is the passage from a corrupt humanity to a new one, from sin to grace and from slavery to freedom. It prevents us from making any of these realities merely private or internal.

"Liberation" is a word rich in connotations for Latin Americans who have struggled to throw off first the domination of Spain and Portugal and now the oppressive power of the first world. It has immediate ties with the revolutionary movements that have been major creative forces in shaping the history of the region. It would seem that the concept of "liberation" takes priority over the symbol of exodus: liberation would seem to set the interpretation of the exodus event into the Latin American context. (One might argue from a different perspective that the exodus was not a revolutionary restructuring of an oppressive society but an exit from one.)

Liberation is a much better term than "development," which was widely used during the 1950's and 1960's to characterize the region. "Development" masked the fact that the first world profited by keeping the rest of the world in an enforced dependency, and that parallel conditions for economic development did not exist in the poorer regions, which could make them examples of capitalist economies at a more primitive stage of growth. The hierarchy of the Roman Catholic Church confirmed the use of the term liberation and used it more and more in pastoral writings after the historic conference at Medellín in 1968. Out of this context, the term liberation may lose some of its connotations and become a less powerful metaphor, especially for political movements in the first world.

We must first see the exodus as an example of the connection between creation and salvation. It points to the goal of the liberating process, the creation of a new type of humanity, one unburdened from the exploitation of present social structures. The exodus created a people where one did not exist; it was also a this-worldly act of salvation that embraced and transformed the whole human reality of the freed slaves. From the perspective of Deutero-Isaiah, creation itself was a salvific act of God. Both the exodus and the exile are acts of recreation of the people through a salvific political action. Gutierrez writes, "Yahweh will be remembered throughout the history of Israel by this act which inaugurates its history, a history which is a recreation. The God who makes the cosmos from chaos is the same God who leads Israel from alienation to liberation."[9]

Jesus Christ brings creation and salvation to a new and unexpected fulfillment. The prologue of John and the Christological hymns of Ephesians 2 and Colossians 1 proclaim that all things were created in Christ and saved in Christ. His work creates a new humanity, so radical is his salvation. Christ saved humanity not only from sin but also from all its consequences, including injustice and hatred. When Christians struggle against these same forces, they enter into the continuation of Christ's creative, salvific work. "To work, to transform this world," writes Gutierrez, "is to become a man and to build the human community; it is also to save."[10] Gutierrez does not equate political liberation with the radical liberation from sin that comes only from grace. But he does hold that there is a single salvific process we must enter by struggling to eradicate society's injustice. This is not all of salvation or the Kingdom—but it is a part.[11]

*The Prophets' Promises*

God's final deliverance promised by the prophets is the second key to understanding the exodus. These promises propel history forward in a more humane direction just as utopian visions animate political hopes and energies. "The Bible," writes Gutierrez, "presents eschatology as the driving force of salvific history radically oriented toward the future." The prophets would not allow Israel to spiritualize these promises or wait passively for God to bring them about. "The prophets announce a kingdom of peace," Gutierrez states. "But peace presupposes the establishment of justice. . . . It presupposes the defense of the rights of the poor, punishment of the oppressors, a life free from the fear of being enslaved by others, the liberation of the oppressed."[12] The prophets called for a radical break with the past and for a new exodus for Israel which could come about only if Israel addressed the social evils of the day. The Church in our time must first *denounce* the existing contradictions in society with the vehemence of prophetic indictment before it can credibly *announce* the Gospel.

Liberation theology has made a major contribution to Christian awareness of social sin. The Old Testament prophets condemned not only personal sin but especially the structures of injustice that perpetuated human enslavement. "But in the liberation approach," explains Gutierrez, "sin . . . is regarded as a social, historical fact, the absence of brotherhood and love in relationships among men. . . . Sin is evident in oppressive structures. . . ."[13] If the reality of sin is structured into our world, the only genuine redemption is one that addresses sin in all its systematic consequences. God's radical liberation of humanity from sin, therefore, is linked intrinsically to political liberation.

Jesus Christ gives new meaning to the eschatological promises of the Old Testament by pointing to a future total reconciliation. He also liberates us from sin by a social reconciliation because he leads us into the believing community. "Christ introduces us by the gift of his Spirit into communion with God and with all men," writes Gutierrez. "More precisely, it is *because* he introduces us into this communion, into a continuous search for its fullness, that he conquers sin—which is the negation of love—and all its consequences."[14] The struggle for justice removes some of the conditions that hinder the full communion of God with men and women.

The third clue to understanding the exodus is found in the Old Testament's teachings that God is closely committed to the people, even identified with the neighbor in need. Gutierrez' belief is that any contact with God must be mediated through serving the needy neighbor. No immediate knowledge of or intimate contact with God is possible apart from the *anawim* with whom God chooses to identify. Yahweh proved to be Emmanuel, God-with-us, first in the wanderings through the desert and the ark of the covenant, then in the glory that filled Solomon's temple in Jerusalem. Jeremiah and Hosea teach that "to know Yahweh, which in biblical language is equivalent to saying to love Yahweh, *is* to establish just relationships among men, it *is* to recognize the rights of the poor," asserts Gutierrez. "The God of biblical revelation is known through interhuman justice. When justice does not exist, God is not known; he is absent."[15]

Once again Jesus Christ fulfills this Old Testament theme. Jesus is the temple of God, the neighbor who is the prime sacrament of our encounter with God. Jesus so identifies himself with the needy that we will be judged by our response to the sick, hungry, thirsty and imprisoned (Mt 25:31–45). Incarnation has a profound moral significance. Because Christ is incarnate in the neighbor's needs, we are called to an active and productive love that seeks out the neighbor, just as the Good Samaritan went out of his way to aid the man beaten by robbers. "Our encounter with the Lord occurs in our encounter with men," explains Gutierrez, "especially in the encounter with those whose human features have been disfigured by oppression, despoliation, and alienation."[16] Gutierrez calls for contemplative and sacramental prayer to nourish this service of the neighbor. He does not seem to be so radically horizontal as José Miranda, who insisted in his *Marx and the Bible* that absolutely no personal contact with God is possible except in the actual accomplishment of social transformation.[17]

Gutierrez' theology is grounded in Old Testament themes, perhaps because the Hebrew Scriptures offer a larger sweep of history and a more sustained experience of society than the New Testament. Christ fulfills the patterns of God's action but does not alter them significantly. In Gutierrez' theology, Scripture is interpreted in a manner that supports a theological and social strategy relevant to the Latin American situation. A different theology would interpret the exodus in a manner that might draw opposing moral conclusions about revolutionary violence. John Howard Yoder cites the exodus as support for his Mennonite pacifism. He contends that in the exodus, Israel learned that Yahweh, not they themselves, was Lord of history. Yahweh would deliver them from the Egyptians in his own way and time. He refers to Exodus 14:13: "For the Egyptians whom you see today you shall never see again. The Lord will fight for you, and you have only to be still." This forms for Yoder the obligatory pattern for Christian political action in history: Christians are called to struggle non-violently against institutional oppression but must leave the results to God rather than try to make history turn out "right."[18] This interpretation of exodus is vindicated by the example of Jesus, the victorious Lamb who was slain.

The adequacy of either interpretation of exodus cannot be determined by citing biblical texts. It must be tested by examining the theological and ethical presuppositions that underlie the interpretation of the exodus event. We must also inquire about the selection of material: What does the author omit from the Bible? This question may be just as relevant as asking what the author includes. For example, Gutierrez rarely refers to the Gospel of John or the Letters of Paul. Is this because their focus is too narrow for his purposes, or does he want to avoid wrestling with some of their social messages (like the Johannine preference for loving members of the community rather than the hostile "world")? Another question regarding method involves the direction of theological interpretation: Should Christ be the principle for interpreting the Old Testament or vice versa? More recent liberation theologians have concentrated more on the story of Jesus as the starting point for their reflections.

### Liberation and the Kingdom: Some Cautions

Without identifying them, Gutierrez carefully connects political liberation and God's liberation of us from sin. The Gospel does not provide us with concrete political strategies, but it does give us a vision of a possible future that corresponds with God's promises. Gutierrez does not fall into the trap of the early twentieth century proponents of the social gospel who too readily equated democratic reform with the arrival of God's Kingdom. Witness the thesis implied in Walter Rauschenbusch's book title *Christianizing the Social Order.*[19]

The concept of liberation has three interdependent meanings for Gutierrez: "political liberation, the liberation of man throughout history, liberation from sin and admission to communion with God."[20] The first process relies on scientific analysis of the structures of oppression and a determination to transform them. Even if this is not the whole of salvation, it does have salvific significance because it attacks the manifestations of selfishness that hinder the coming of the Kingdom. The second meaning depends on a vision of humanity that encourages people to take responsibility for their own destiny and inspires them with the hope of a just society. It is product of "utopian thinking" and its projection into history. The third concept of liberation is not human achievement but the work of God, who liberates from sin. It is thus on the level of faith rather than social analysis or utopian visions. We must see these three processes working together; as Gutierrez explains: "Not only is the growth of the Kingdom not reduced to temporal progress; because of the Word accepted in faith, we see that the fundamental obstacle to the Kingdom, which is sin, is also the root of all misery and injustice; we see that the very meaning of the growth of the Kingdom is also the ultimate precondition for a just society and a new man."[21]

The connecting link between denouncing present oppression and announcing the coming Kingdom is the utopian vision of a new humanity. Unfortunately, Gutierrez fails to clarify this vision sufficiently for it to ground a theory of justice. This is a significant omission because, in a time of revolution, certain moral standards must apply lest the social transformation be corrupted by vindictive violence and retribution. We need some clarity about what is normatively human in order to develop a theory of justice: What are the inalienable rights, even of one's enemies? What guarantees can be cited for the protection of equality, solidarity and liberty in the new society? Gutierrez does not, and I think cannot, supply a theory of justice because his ethics is so vague, corresponding as it does to the vague vision of the new humanity. Some liberationists dismiss concern over a theory of justice as premature. They argue that one can only discover what the new humanity is when social structures have been radically altered to produce this new type of person.

Gutierrez' theology is influenced by a Marxist view of class struggle, which he finds is the only adequate way to describe the deeply divided Latin America polity. The Church performs a disservice when it uses the rhetoric of Church unity to mask the antithetical interests of the rich and exploited. This gives a novel meaning to the Gospel command to love one's enemies. "One loves the oppressor by liberating them from themselves," Gutierrez writes. "But this cannot be achieved except by resolutely opting for the oppressed, that is, by combatting the oppressing class. It must be a real and effective combat, not hate."[22] Armed revolution cannot be ruled out if this is the only way to liberate the powerful from their power to oppress others. Ironically, a pacifist stance would fail to love the exploiter effectively. Gutierrez does not discuss the biblical witness of Jesus' suffering as fulfilling Deutero-Isaiah's prophecies of the servant who is led to death like a lamb to the slaughter and relinquishes his hopes into the Lord's hands (cf. Is 49:4–7; 53:1–12). Perhaps this can instruct individual suffering and failure, but not social struggles.

The distinctive witness of Jesus is not central to Gutierrez' account: not the story of Jesus but certain theological doctrines interpret his moral meaning. Subsequent liberation theologies have accorded a more crucial role to the story of Jesus. Leonardo Boff, for example, indicates that Jesus provides an example that is normative for any political strategy that Christians adopt. "Christian faith does not prescribe a specific concrete program," he writes, "but demands a specific attitude which must be present in any practical action or any position taken. Therefore, if Christians aim at taking power because this appears to them to be the imperative of the moment, they must do so not as domination but as service and not in a spirit of vengeance but as a reconciliatory solution to discrimination in social structure."[23]

One major liberation theologian does not see any regulative role for the example of Jesus today. Juan Luis Segundo in *The Liberation of Theology* states that circumstances are decisive for moral choice. We need to develop our own "ideologies" under the guidance of the Spirit but not be tied down to the historical approach of Jesus. "When Jesus talked about freely proffered love and non-resistance to evil," he writes, "he was faced with the same problem of filling the void between his conception of God (or perhaps that of the first Christian community) and the problems existing in his age. In short, we are dealing here with another ideology, not the content of faith itself." Segundo justifies this by appealing to the Johannine doctrine of the Paraclete, who will continue to instruct the disciples in ways Jesus could not in his own life (Jn 16:12–16). He then draws the obvious conclusion: "This view of the matter gives liberation theology greater freedom to move, in principle, through the Scriptures and to work with the faith."[24] One wonders whether anyone can so confidently distinguish between outdated ideology and "faith itself." Certainly the New Testament does not provide a normative pattern for Christian identity for Segundo, though it does for most Latin American liberationists.

A more developed ethics is needed in Gutierrez' theology and those of many other liberation theologians. Perhaps the pressing demands of their situation make this critical task seem superfluous, but it would prevent them from moving too quickly from the Bible to politics without passing through ethics. Revolutionary zeal and compassion do not ensure justice in the world that follows the revolution, as the transition from Marx to Lenin to Stalin tragically demonstrates. Scripture teaches that sin will never be fully eradicated from history until its end point, and that persistent sinful tendencies of individuals can sabotage the most carefully managed social systems.

A final point in which Marx influences Gutierrez' case is his treatment of the poor as though they were a moral proletariat. The salvation of humanity passes through them; they bear the meaning of history and "inherit the Kingdom (Jas 2:5)."[25] "The future of history belongs to the poor and exploited," asserts Gutierrez. "True liberation will be the work of the oppressed themselves; in them the Lord saves history."[26] The poor play the same role for Gutierrez as the proletarian masses do for Marx. They are the class that holds the seeds of the future; they have the latent energy to transform existing structures because they experience the contradictions of such structures most fully. It is undeniable that the Bible mandates a special concern for the poor as proof of fidelity to the covenant with the Lord; it does not seem to confer on them a privileged position of greater wisdom as if they hold the key to social progress. There is the

danger of romanticizing marginated groups because they are uncon-
taminated by the usage of power. However, the poor are sinners, too,
and their assumption of power may contaminate them in turn. Had
Gutierrez treated the fall or the role "sin" plays as a dynamic in
Paul's theology, we might have a more adequate picture of individual
sinfulness to complement his insights on social sin.

## II.  Letty Russell and Phyllis Trible: Liberation Theology and Feminism

The work of Gutierrez and other liberation theologians has been
adapted by both blacks and women in American society to address
their own situations of injustice. Letty Russell uses Scripture in a
thematic way to rediscover neglected images of God and provide a
theology of servanthood as the basis for reforming the Church. Phyllis Trible employs a different method in the same cause. Her literary
analysis of three Old Testament works unearths a new and liberating
interpretation of human sexuality.

Both authors tackle the problem the Bible poses for many feminists—its "patriarchal" character, reflected in its descriptions of cultures in which women were submissive to men. Some feminists have
jettisoned the entire biblical tradition as irredeemably sexist and
turned to other ancient religions for female images of the deity. Trible concedes that any attempt to eliminate the male-dominated character of Scripture would be both futile and dishonest, but a feminist
perspective can still be brought to the text with positive results.
"Clearly, the patriarchal stamp of Scripture is permanent," she
writes. "But just as clearly, interpretation of its content is forever
changing, since new occasions teach new duties and contexts alter
texts, liberating them from frozen constructions. Moving across cultures and centuries, then, the Bible informed a feminist perspective,
and, correspondingly, a feminist perspective enlightened the Bible."[27]
Russell intends to search for a "usable past" in the biblical tradition
to illuminate feminist consciousness and keep it as a leaven in the on-
going tradition of faith. Although some reject the Bible, she insists
that "those who would do Christian theology cannot abandon the
story of Jesus of Nazareth."[28]

Every Christian ethics has an implicit Christology that suits its moral and theological foundations, and Russell's work is no exception. Jesus provides the most important clues for the authentic humanity both men and women seek. Not only did Jesus reveal what true personhood could be, but he also helped all to understand their full humanity. His life and ministry displayed certain qualities that are often stereotyped as "feminine" in our culture—love, compassion and caring.[29] Every theology stumbles over some aspect of Jesus of Nazareth; for feminists it is the scandal of particularity in his maleness. Nevertheless, "for women and men alike, Jesus embodies in his life, death and resurrection what a truly human being (*anthropos*) might be like. One who would love and live and suffer for love of God and for others. He was not just a male (*anēr*); he was for us all . . . . He was the second humanity (Adam) and showed both parts of humanity, male and female, both the cost and promise of freedom (1 Cor 15:45)."[30]

Feminist scholars have given us a groundbreaking interpretation of the Genesis creation accounts. Trible provides a careful exegesis of the metaphor of the "image of God" (Gen 1:26) which humanity, male and female, are created to be. It is not the male who is the image of God, but humanity in its sexual differentiation and unity. While this metaphor preserves the transcendence of God, it does give us a significant clue to God's indescribable reality. "God is neither male nor female, nor a combination of the two," Trible states. "And yet, detecting divine transcendence in human reality requires human clues. Unique among them, according to our poem, is sexuality."[31]

Although she agrees with Trible that the Genesis account grounds the radical equality of the sexes, Russell reads the complementarity of human creation in a somewhat different fashion. For her the traditionally "feminine" images of servant and helper ascribed to God in the Old Testament ought to guide men and women in their mutual help and obedience. "As we have seen," she writes, "the Genesis etiological myths are designed to explain the relationship of polarity and attraction between men and women, but their principal focus is on the possibility of reciprocity. Man and woman were created to be in relationship with God and one another. Servanthood, not sexuality, is the primary bearer of God's image."[32]

Liberation in a Christian context is liberation *for* service to others, modeled on the life style of Jesus. We cannot dwell only on what we desire to be liberated *from* lest the theology be no more than the ethos of an oppressed group. It becomes an ethics when it states what it is accountable for and what the principles are to which it will be responsible. Russell argues for *partnership,* for new forms of genuinely reciprocal service between women and men. She develops this notion from the controversial New Testament household mandates of service. In neither the Old nor New Testament is the role of servant seen to be one of inferiority or submission. The Christological hymn of Philippians 2, which celebrates the self-emptying of Jesus into servanthood, becomes the norm. "This service to others on behalf of God was not a form of subordination to other people," states Russell, "but rather a free offering of self and acceptance of service and love in return (Lk 7:36–50; 8:1–3; 10:38–42)."[33] In relationships of true partnership, women would be freed to serve and be served without fear of subordination or loss of identity.

This vision of partnership demands basic changes in roles of ministry and organization in the Church. While the Latin Americans work from the basis of the Church to refashion society and remove the oppression of "national security" dictatorships, Russell focuses on the liberation of the Church itself. "Liberation theologians," she argues, "cannot ignore this task of *subverting the church into being the church.* . . ."[34] Access to ordination and leadership, use of inclusive language in worship, partnership in Church organization, and critique of sexist values in our culture are just some of the tasks to be undertaken.

Trible takes a more exegetical approach than Russell, but her stance does have liberationist implications. She uses literary criticism rather than social analysis as she unearths images of God and interpretations of human sexuality that serve as a critique of misogyny. After treating the creation account as a love poem that turns into a tragedy through the fall, she turns to the Song of Songs and Ruth for illustrations of biblical views of sexuality. When the Song of Songs is read through the lens of Genesis 2–3, we discover a celebration of human love. "Born to mutuality and harmony," she writes, "a man and a woman live in a garden where nature and history unite to celebrate the one flesh of sexuality. . . . In this setting, there is no male dominance, no female subordination, and no stereotyping of either sex. Specifically, the portrayal of the woman defies the connotations of 'second sex.' "[35]

The story of Ruth and Boaz is another example of a balanced view of sexuality. It is a human comedy in which the female lead characters take surprising initiatives. They work out their own salvation as God works in them. "Together they are women in culture," writes Trible, "women against culture, and women transforming culture."[36] Although she only alludes to the implications of her exegesis, Trible offers the reader a well-documented case for fresh views of human sexuality and complementary equality. Hers is an excellent example of the work still to be done by most liberation theologies—the exegesis of biblical texts rather than the mere use of the Bible for illustration or rhetorical support for a movement. More attention to the "then" meaning of Scripture will make them better theological evidence for the "now" meaning that liberation theology strives to describe today.

Liberation theology insists on action as the fulcrum for changing the moral agent. Even though it does not always claim the competence to prescribe the practical solutions to injustice, it highlights the attitudes necessary for social transformation. The next three chapters focus more on the transformation of the moral agent and the believing community. How do the symbols and perspectives of Scripture take root in the Christian? How does the person change so that the proverbial heart of stone becomes a perceptive and responsive heart of flesh? Both the new moral theology and liberation thought moved from the human situation to Scripture. The next chapters will show how insights gained from biblical perspectives illumine and redefine the human situation. How does the distinctive Christian viewpoint penetrate moral problems to reveal and enable the believers' response?

# 4

# Response to Revelation

In this third approach to the use of Scripture, the moral question is translated into a theological one. Instead of asking, "What ought I to do?" we must first ask, "What is God doing in my situation?" The answer will not come from any direct command of God or from a reasonable assessment of what is normatively human, but from a process of discernment guided by key biblical symbols and perspectives. Discernment is an exploratory way of knowing in the concrete which uses imaginative and affective criteria to discover what the appropriate response should be to God's action.

God does not work so immediately or call so directly in this approach as in that of Barth and Bultmann. Nor does the Christian detect God's will by looking primarily to the natural patterns of human flourishing. Both of the previous models advocated a prescriptive use of moral norms—that is, they were specific mandates calling for obedience. Here moral norms are less apodictic. They are employed illuminatively; they cast light on the situation but are subordinate to an exercise of the "reasoning heart," which uses the imagination to explore the signs of the times. Therefore, the most significant resources Scripture can provide for the moral life are the symbols and images that can help us interpret what is occurring.

The main proponent of this approach is the American theologian H. Richard Niebuhr, whose writings have influenced all of the authors considered here and in the next three chapters. Niebuhr was of German Calvinist origins and the brother of the more widely known Reinhold Niebuhr, whose prolific reflections on social issues

70

shaped Christian ethics in America in mid-century. H. Richard's output was less voluminous than his brother's, but his acute analysis of moral experience has made him a dominant figure in the field in the twenty years since his death. Bruce C. Birch and Larry L. Rasmussen combined their expertise in Old Testament and ethics to produce the other work we will investigate, *The Predicament of the Prosperous.* [1] They deliberately employ Niebuhr's method to envision the response wealthy Christians must make in a world of scarcity.

Niebuhr, like the Catholic theologians Fuchs and Schüller, gives priority to the religious transformation of the moral agent. However, he connects the resulting "fundamental orientation" of the agent with the actual practice of decision-making more clearly than they do. Charles Curran is an example of this Catholic appropriation of Niebuhr. He accepts an overall ethical model of responsibility to God, but on the practical level he supplements that approach with a strong reliance on moral norms and consequences. His "mixed consequentialism" considers an action in light of its consequences, including those accruing to the agent, to determine the moral rightness of that action. [2] Most Catholic and many Protestant ethicists want to use moral norms and goals to complement Niebuhr's discernment through biblical symbols. Whether this vitiates his method is debatable; he states that a legal or consequential approach to ethics is inadequate for a Christian response. [3]

## I.  H. Richard Niebuhr: Interpreting Events

The best known example of Niebuhr's discernment was his series of articles in *The Christian Century* in 1942 and 1943. He asked a question that upset many of the journal's readers: "What is God doing in the war?" The two biblical themes that guided his discernment are indicated in the titles "War as the Judgment of God" and "War as Crucifixion." [4] We will use these articles to explain his approach to ethics. First we will see how events are interpreted in a context of faith to indicate an appropriate response. Then we will examine the moral agent to show how a new self-understanding is the pre-condition for discernment.

Isaiah's analysis of the invading Assyrians provided Niebuhr with the model for prophetic interpretation of the tragic events of the

Second World War. The prophet could detect a different meaning in the invasion than the proud boasts of Sennacherib. For the prophet, the Lord has a different design:

> Woe to Assyria! My rod in anger,
>     my staff in wrath.
> Against an impious nation I send him,
>     and against a people under my wrath I order him
> To seize plunder, carry off loot,
>     and tread them down like the mud of the streets.
> But this is not what he intends,
>     nor does he have this in mind;
> Rather it is in his heart to destroy,
>     to make an end of nations not a few (Is 10:5-7).

Isaiah called for a constructive response to this national emergency because he interpreted the events in a context of faith and saw them as Yahweh's call to Israel to repent. He discounts Sennacherib's arrogance, which takes credit for all his successes; the imperialist is merely a tool in the Lord's hands: "Will the axe boast against him who hews with it? . . . As if a rod could sway him who lifts it, or a staff him who is not wood!" (v. 15). From the conqueror's standpoint, he is the cause of his own victories; from the cowering Israelites' point of view, he is a threat to national survival; to the prophet, he is the instrument of God's saving judgment on faithless Israel.

The prophet has a privileged standpoint because he is committed to seek out the action of the one universal Lord in this and all events of life. If we pay attention only to the finite actors on the scene, we will miss the more profound significance of what is happening. Jesus adopted this same standpoint when faced with the threat of crucifixion. "To see the act of God in war," writes Niebuhr, "is to stand where Isaiah stood when he discerned that Assyria was the rod of divine anger and where Jesus stood when he saw in the crucifixion not Pilate's nor the Jews' activity but that of the Father who gave Pilate the power to crucify and whose will rather than Pilate's or Jesus' was being done."[5] An observer could try to make sense out of the cross or the Assyrian invasion from many perspectives, but only the perspective of responsible faith could detect the One who was acting through the intentions of the many finite agents. They may have their own designs, but the Lord works them into a larger pattern that they know nothing of.

## The Standpoint of Christian Faith

Events are always understood from one standpoint or another. Niebuhr cautioned that all of our judgments are relative to a particular cultural and historical standpoint. Taking into account this perspective and its limitations for viewing the event is necessary even in religion. The Scriptures themselves show various perspectives we move into when we join the community of faith; philosophically speaking, we may make valid statements about the Absolute but we cannot claim these absolutely unconditioned. Note the shift from natural law and its perspectives. We have moved from considering *natures* in the context of being to a more cautious twentieth century framework. Here the focus is on *events* in the context of the history that gives them meaning.

Events, whether of massive scope like a world war or limited like the death of a friend, can be read in many different ways. Their meaning is not readily available for public inspection like a label listing the ingredients in a can of stew. We must actively try to locate these events in various frameworks of meaning to illuminate the various qualities inherent in them. We must always *interpret* events, literally "make sense" out of them by locating them in different contexts. The death of a friend can be described by a pathologist, but we reject that interpretation as final. Ultimately, the Christian will try to understand such a loss in light of the cross and resurrection of Jesus. Then the death itself will become symbolic of larger meanings, of God's fidelity and our own mortality. We turn to revelation because we believe that its central symbols will reveal the deepest significance of such events.

Different contexts of meaning lead to morally diverse, and even incompatible, descriptions of a given action. For example, the problem of abortion is not what to do about it but how to describe it. Is it the taking of a human life? Is it an exercise of the right of privacy by the pregnant woman over her own reproductive capacities? Or should Christians describe the challenge of abortion as a call to welcome children into the community as gifts and not threats, as Stanley Hauerwas urges? Only from a common perspective does any moral response seem to be adequate. Niebuhr is not so confident as natural law proponents that our common humanity offers such a unifying perspective.

What is the most adequate standpoint for interpreting the tragic events of war? That of the detached observer who prescinds from personal factors for the sake of objectivity is obviously inadequate. We must stand as persons and participants within this common history if we are to gauge the full human cost of war. The Christian tradition sees conflicts in continuity with the history of Israel and Jesus, susceptible to the same interpretation they made to disclose the underlying divine intention. We use scriptural symbols to discover that underlying action of God and respond to it; it is all part of one history. "Faith cannot get to God save through historic experience as reason cannot get to nature save through sense-experience," wrote Niebuhr in the 1941 classic *The Meaning of Revelation.*[6] We have no access to the objective qualities of the divine being; nevertheless, the Christian tradition has grasped the characteristic actions of God in its own history, the revelation of who God is through what he does. Scripture is the normative witness to that revelation in history.

The faithful person uses the patterns central to Scripture to look for the continuing manifestation of God in contemporary events. "Thus prophets," Niebuhr states, "for whom the revelation of God was connected with his mighty acts in the deliverance of Israel from bondage, found the marks of that God's working in the histories of all nations. The Christian community must turn in like manner from the revelation of the universal God in a limited history to the recognition of his rule and providence in all events of all times and communities."[7] This is done through symbolic, not causal, analysis. God is neither the efficient cause of everything that occurs, nor the predeterminer of destinies, the author of a fixed script we unwittingly act out. God's action is described through biblical symbols and metaphors. In all events, he governs, judges and redeems in a manner analogous to his classic actions described in Scripture. Since the memory of the exodus aided the prophets of the exile in interpreting the seventy years of the Babylonian captivity as a second exodus,

Niebuhr is justified in using the symbols of judgment and crucifixion to make sense of the tragedy of World War II.

## Discerning God's Action in the War

God *governs* in part through the limitations of our own finitude, *judges* by calling us to repentance, and *redeems* by bringing to light new possibilities of reconciliation that were hidden to our despairing hearts. He does all of this simultaneously. Hence, his judgment cannot be dismissed as penal and vindictive, as if it could be abstracted from his gracious governance and redemption. Divine justice "is never merely punishment for sins," Niebuhr explains, "as though God were concerned simply to restore the balance between men by making those suffer who have inflicted suffering, but . . . it is always primarily punishment of sinners who are to be chastened and changed in the character which produced the sinful acts."[8] When he viewed the war through the lens of biblical judgment, Niebuhr concluded that God was on neither side, that the relative culpability of various nations ought not to be judged by us, and that the war must not be fought under the assumption that the Allies were God's agents of retribution. No wonder his readers objected so strenuously! Niebuhr did not proceed to list specific rules to dictate moral response. Rather, he probed the attitudes of both pacifists and "coercionists" and found them inadequate. He limited himself to suggesting a new spirit and context for interpreting the war.

Only the context of the central symbol of the New Testament, the cross of Christ, can render intelligible the suffering of the innocent millions caught in the path of the war machines. Like war, the cross was a mixture of justice and injustice performed by those who saw it only as their duty. Neither a theory of vindictive justice nor the purity of non-involvement can grasp the meaning of the cross or the war. The cross points to an order of grace that comes through the vicarious suffering of the innocent to those who are guilty, not to a world order where good is always rewarded and evil punished. The suffering of the guiltless becomes a call to religious conversion, an act of grace in the paradox of tragedy. Niebuhr writes:

> Interpreted through the cross of Jesus Christ the suffering
> of the innocent is seen not as the suffering of temporal men

but of the eternal victim "slain from the foundations of the world." If the Son of God is being crucified in this war along with the malefactors—and he is being crucified on many an obscure hill—then the graciousness of God, the self-giving love, is more manifest here than in all the years of peace.[9]

When viewed in the context of retributive justice, the appropriate response to war would be righteous anger toward the guilty. From the perspective of the cross, however, the fitting response is a repentance that acknowledges our own complicity in permitting injustice and turns to the renewing call of God.

## The Key Symbol for Christians

Jesus Christ is the key "symbolic form" through which Christians discern the meaning of what is going on. He was the supremely responsible human who sought the action of God in all events, from the fall of a sparrow to the betrayal of Judas. We are called to imitate not the details of his external manner of life but his loyalty, by responding in the many events of our lives to the One who is acting in and through them. He is the "Rosetta stone" that unlocks the hieroglyphs to disclose God's hidden presence.[10] Jesus responds to God not as the Great Predestiner, but rather as though "his action is more like that of the great wise leader who uses even the meanness of his subjects to promote the public welfare."[11]

Christ enables us to be converted so that we can move from viewing the ultimate context as God the Void or even God the Enemy to God the Friend. Other sources of moral wisdom are necessary to interpret events. Jesus is not the only principle of moral wisdom for the Christian, even if his life and person are indispensable. Convinced of the historical relativity of all religious statements, including Scripture, Niebuhr does not call us to follow the specific mandates of Jesus' teaching. Rather, we use the character of Jesus witnessed in Scripture as our criterion for discerning. The Christian "tests the spirits to see if among all the forces that move within him, his societies, the human mind itself, there can be uniting, a healing, a knowing, a whole-making spirit, a Holy Spirit. And he can do so only with the aid of the image, the symbol of Christ. 'Is there a Christ-like spirit there?' "[12] The cause of reconciliation is central to the character and mission of Jesus; the qualities of this reconciliation guide discernment.

What compels believers to search out this universal activity of God? Such a quest is absolutely necessary if we are to believe in *one* God and have the integrity of *one* self. If God reigns in certain regions of experience but is absent from others, what deity reigns there? "To deny that God is in the war," writes Niebuhr, "is for the monotheist equivalent to the denial of God's universality and unity—to the denial that God is God. . . . To look for God's judgment is to affirm as radical monotheists that there is no person, no situation, no event in which the opportunity to serve God is not present."[13] If God is absent from part of our experience, then we are dualists and not monotheists, and our response will take a dualistic form—one response to the opponent or the absurd situation and another to God. It is not easy to seek the universal in every particular and respond to that One with trust and loyalty. Possessing the Scriptures is no guarantee that this discernment will be correct. Yet only this exploration of meaning will enable us to have some integrity in our very selves. The alternative is the fragmented self that is accountable to numerous deities and has no more integrity than a chameleon. Patriotism, professionalism, ambition, pleasure, reputation, anxiety, fashion and the rest form the pantheon in which the fragmented self worships.

## II.  Interpreting the Self

Revelation guides a second form of discernment because it aids the believer in attaining a new self-understanding. One of Niebuhr's most original contributions to ethics was his insight that the question "Who am I?" must be asked even before we ask "What ought I to do?" Self-understanding defines the perspective of the moral agent. We need to acknowledge that perspective because it enters into all of our descriptions and perceptions of the situation. Not only do we bring our own distinctive point of view to each situation, but we also have a unique future that will be shaped by the decisions we make in the present. Discernment seeks to discover both what God is doing in these events and choices and what they will do to me. We become what we do, so the individual must ask, "Do I want to become the kind of person who does this sort of action? Does it fit in with who I want to be?"

The change of behavior that religious conversion effects is root- ed in the transformation of self-understanding it demands. Niebuhr stands with Augustine, Calvin and Jonathan Edwards in asserting that the moral agent is spontaneously self-centered. In all actions, the ego is center stage, the star of its own show. On its own, the self is unable to see experience in any other way. When my race or class or profession becomes the center of value, it is merely egotism ex- panded. Only the gracious revelation that the whole of reality is trustworthy can unself the agent and evoke a universal loyalty to off- set the innate parochialism of the human spirit. The root sin of hu- manity is this self-love, which expresses itself in defensiveness of personal interests and exclusion of others. The necessary condition for moral conversion, therefore, must be religious conversion to rede- fine the self.

The New Testament seems to agree with this. Matthew counsels that we cannot expect good fruit from bad trees, nor figs from bram- ble bushes (Mt 7:16–18). Moral reformation either goes to the root or is futile. True to this parable, the Reformers taught that the agent must be healed by the free grace of Christ, radically transformed so that the tree is no longer diseased but fruitful of good works. Most moral philosophies—and too much of Catholic moral theology—ig- nored this insight, bracketing the transformation and healing of fun- damental dispositions in favor of the more manageable task of specifying proper norms of conduct.

## The Reasoning Heart and Its Symbols

There is no set self-understanding given to any individual; each must achieve his or her unique identity through interaction with oth- ers. "Self" is a relational term because our societies shape our per- sonal identity. First the family and then the expectation of the larger society force the emerging self to conform to their customs and ex- pectations. As our unique history develops, we find ourselves looking for some intelligible pattern, some self-consistency to guide our choices. We cannot derive this integrity from any general concept or idea because they fail to fit our unique and multivalent history. The detachment of theory is inadequate: this is *our* history and we must adopt the standpoint of the participants in it. Niebuhr states, "The heart must reason; the participating self cannot escape the necessity of looking for pattern and meaning in its life and relations."[14] The heart reasons with symbols, personal images that organize its deep affective dispositions. Imagination provides the meaningful structures that discover order in the affections. Scripture provides these personal images, which can revolutionize the self-understanding of the person. "The heart reasons with the aid of revelation," writes Niebuhr, because the heart uses the images provided by the community of faith to discover an intelligible pattern in its own experience.[15]

The discovery and surprise of conversion are these break-throughs of the imagination, turning points that shatter an entire world and illuminate a new one. Consider the parable of the prophet Nathan, which catches King David. As the Second Book of Samuel relates, David killed off Uriah so he could take to himself Bathsheba, his wife. Nathan tells the story of a rich man who ignored his own flocks and herds and stole the "one little ewe lamb" of a poor neighbor to feast on with a visitor. David in righteous anger swears, "As the Lord lives, the man who had done this merits death . . . because he has done this and has had no pity" (2 Sam 12:5). Nathan then says to David, "That man is you!" He exposes the king to himself as well as to his court. The tissue of rationalization and self-deception is torn away: David has become this grasping, unmerciful man. Without the image of Nathan's parable, the truth could not have appeared nor could that depth of repentance been engendered. "Revelation," asserts Niebuhr, "does not accomplish the work of conversion; the reasoning heart must search out memory and bring to light forgotten deeds. But without the revelatory image this work does not seem possible."[16]

## *Story and Self-Understanding*

To gain this sense of self, the imagination needs an image that can fit a history, a personal character that emerges through time. It needs the particular imaginative device of the *story*. Only stories can convey the dramatic unity appropriate to a unique lifetime: the intel-

ligible pattern of character emerges through the twists and turns of
the plot. The prime image of the heart is "a dramatic action in which
the self is the protagonist."[17] We need to move from this spontaneously narcissistic drama into a different story. So the prophet Nathan, while still pointing the accusatory finger at David, recounts all
that the Lord has done for him. How could he spurn the Lord who
has been so gracious to him? Conversion implies moving into a different story, making the common memory and tradition of the Christian community our own. This story now becomes our story, but we
are no longer the center of the narrative.

Not only is a new self-understanding discerned in this change of
story, but the personal reality of God is self-disclosed. The goodness
of God is no longer an ideal guiding our journey from afar. In genuine religious conversion, Niebuhr reveals, the surprise is that "we
sought a good to love and were found by a good that loves us."[18] The
story of God's dealings with Israel and Jesus provides the pattern for
this new self-understanding and reveals that the principal Actor of
that story is also the principal Actor of our own story. Conversion
takes root as the self reinterprets its own past and future in light of
this self-disclosure of God and responds appropriately. Scripture
provides paradigms for this response. The fifty-first psalm is attribut-
ed to David as his grieving response to Nathan's prophecy. Today
we can enter into that same attitude of repentance guided by the
story and the affections of the psalm: "Have mercy on me, O God,
in your goodness; in the greatness of your compassion wipe out my
offense . . ." (v. 1).

An adequate story for our lives must be able to assimilate sup-
pressed memories and embarrassing images, parts of our histories we
would prefer to forget. It must draw into the unity of the self even
the centrifugal forces of absurdity and death, which threaten to shatter any integrity. Those who confess the truth of the Christian story
experience its adequacy practically, as they respond to the One who
is disclosing himself and interpret more and more of their history
through the lens of that story. "It is progressively validated in the
individual Christian life," states Niebuhr, "as ever new occasions are
brought under its light, as sufferings and sins, as mercies and joys are
understood by its aid."[19] Social corroboration in the confessing com-

munity of what the believer has perceived helps substantiate the original perception. The full truth of the story is attested to by the deepening dialectic between life and revelation. The reasoning heart moves from life experience to communal revelation and back again, progressively grasping the meaning of revelation more richly.

## Conversion Through Revelation

Once we accept the importance of self-understanding in religious ethics, we can recognize in Scripture the role renewed self-understanding has played in our history. Niebuhr refers primarily to the literature of the prophetic tradition. Great prophets were often great poets. We may think they made their impact on Israel by proclaiming the covenant's morality. In reality, they convict Israel more by challenging national self-understanding with powerful imagery. Hosea confronts the nation with the symbol of adultery to indict Israel and reveal the peculiarly personal quality of her infidelity. With his life, the prophet models the long-suffering husband who stays faithful to the marriage covenant while his spouse goes astray with her lovers. Yahweh will frustrate the desires of Israel to bring her back eventually to a new betrothal. Isaiah 40—60 portrays the deliverance of the exiles from Babylon as a new exodus, a homecoming when they would find the Lord as their ancestors had in the wilderness. The God who acts in the present will act "in character," consistent with his saving deeds of the past. Nostalgia looks to an irretrievable past; the prophets proclaim that the same Lord is acting in the present. "The revelation of God is not a possession but an event," Niebuhr asserts, "which happens over and over again when we remember the illuminating center of our history."[20] By recalling that event, we discover God in the present, and progress toward a new self-understanding.

The best portrayal in the New Testament of a person coming to self-understanding is in Paul's Second Letter to the Corinthians. Paul returns constantly to the image of the cross and resurrection of Jesus to interpret the meaning of his own sufferings. His opponents in Corinth have demeaned him for his physical infirmities and the failure of his missionary efforts. With high irony, Paul turns the indictment against them. His sufferings are actually his credentials as a true apostle of Christ. Because he has discerned the presence of God in these events, he is confident that others can do the same. "Brothers," he says, "we do not wish to leave you in the dark about the trouble we had in Asia; we were crushed beyond our strength, even to the point of despairing of life. We were left to feel like men condemned to death so that we might trust, not in ourselves, but in God who raises the dead" (1:8-9). Paul intimates that his own experience is intelligible only in the light of the experience of Jesus; he is somehow being worked into the same pattern.

Even Paul's physical problems testify to this pattern of salvation's central event. His infirmities co-exist with the power of God. "He said to me," Paul states, " 'My grace is enough for you, for in weakness power reaches perfection.' And so I willingly boast of my weaknesses instead, that the power of Christ may rest upon me" (12:9). Paul's struggles are significant in yet another way: they are for the sake of others just as Christ's sufferings were. They are not for his benefit, but for those he serves. "He comforts us in all our afflictions," says Paul, "and thus enables us to comfort those who are in trouble, with the same consolation we have received from him" (1:4). In audacious language, Paul expresses the central pattern of Christian ministry: "Death is at work in us, but life in you" (4:12). The Church has long admired Paul's genius in crafting such images as the body of Christ to revision pastoral problems and evoke the appropriate response. Perhaps even more profound is Paul's gift for a similar imaginative exploration of the depths of Christian experience.

## III.   Selecting the Appropriate Images

A thorny problem arises when we use Scripture as a source of guiding images: How do we select the right ones? Some current writers seem to have abandoned proof-texting for "proof-theming"—selecting biblical images that support moral conclusions they have reached on other grounds. History has shown that fanatics often cloak their delusions in the mantle of inspiration by appealing to convenient biblical precedents. Why not imitate Samson's destruction of the Philistines rather than Moses' deliverance of the people from slavery, since both are in the canonical Scripture? Critics have charged that symbolic discernment by someone like H. Richard Niebuhr yields far different results than when practiced by a deranged zealot or an uncritical partisan of some cause. What criteria can we establish to prevent such distortions of the biblical discernment?

We can only sketch certain criteria for selection that seem to be inherent in Niebuhr's use of Scripture for moral guidance:

1. The appropriate biblical images should be central to the canon of Scripture. Did they function as continuing sources of revelation for the tradition or are they at least consistent with its central images? The exodus, for example, continued to shape Israel's consciousness, while on the other hand the holy war of total annihilation found in Judges does not play this role.

2. The guiding images should convey or be coordinate with a theologically sound image of God. The exodus implies the character of God as Redeemer and Deliverer of captives; the holy war alludes to a vindictive deity of nationalism.

3. The images should be consistent with God's definitive revelation in Jesus Christ. For Christians, the theological center of reference must be the saving event of Christ. Therefore, images from both Testaments must be gauged against the story of Jesus. He is the New Moses who leads God's people from slavery through his own Passover from death to life; the crusading warrior of the holy war is inconsistent with the character of Jesus presented in the New Testament

4. The images should be appropriate to the situation and shed light upon it.

5. Finally, these images should indicate courses of action that concur with the standards of ordinary human morality. Christians may well be called to a way of life that is more

demanding than ordinary morality, but they most assuredly are not called by God to behavior that is patently harmful to themselves or others. This criterion introduces the practice of a public test to check any suspension of the moral law in the name of personal inspiration.[21]

Recall the various sources of Christian ethics: Scripture, tradition, moral philosophy and empirical data. Any coherent argument will draw on all these sources in an integrated way. Our selection of biblical material must be justified by the other sources we use: theological validity in the tradition, consistency with the normative portrait of the human person found in ethics, and relevance to the factual situation as determined by the best empirical analyses available. Biblical authority is too often used to bolster arguments that have not been carefully reasoned with reference to the other sources of Christian ethics.

Niebuhr warns against "evil imaginations of the heart," symbols that send us down false ways and evoke self-centered affections. They obscure the truth of who we are and what we are doing, thus leading to a future not of life, but of death. Evil imaginations of the heart are detected by the consequences they lead to, just as concepts are invalidated by their erroneous results.[22] Apartheid is a classic example of this. The Dutch Reformed settlers of South Africa justified their suppression of the native peoples by invoking the biblical symbol of taking the land of Canaan. Confident that they were the Lord's elect who had been led across the waters into a promised land, they dealt as harshly with the Zulu as Joshua had with the Canaanites. Their descendants still invoke this interpretation to support the deadly system of apartheid.

This use of the symbol of "taking the land" fails the criteria listed above. It is not a central theme of Israel's religious consciousness. It conveys an image of God as more nationalist than universally redemptive. It has no confirmation in the New Testament experience of Jesus. Finally, its consequences are abhorrent to ordinary moral sensibility. Despite its biblical origins, the only truth it reveals is the depth of fear and racial defensiveness that inhabited the Afrikaaners' hearts. Even a casual viewer of some of the current media evangelists will witness a similar uncritical use of biblical material to support the values of American nationalism and commercialism.

## IV. Bruce Birch and Larry Rasmussen: A Plurality of Perspectives

The standpoint provided by the prophetic literature must be supplemented by other standpoints, by perspectives in other forms of biblical literature. Birch and Rasmussen's *The Predicament of the Prosperous* broadens Niebuhr's range of biblical material to show this necessary complementarity. In doing so, they demonstrate that the use of biblical perspectives to guide moral action can be deceptive if only a single set of biblical images dominates our discernment.

Birch and Rasmussen apply Niebuhr's method to the problem of wealthy first world Christians in a world of increasing scarcity. Popular American Christianity has prided itself on prosperity as God's reward for his chosen ones. The radical disparity of wealth and resources in the late twentieth century calls for a national conversion. "History's testimony," they write, "is that the most far-reaching change comes only with the *combination of strong pressures,* from within and without, *and a compelling vision.*"[23] Biblical materials can provide the change of imagery that will facilitate this change of perspective.

American civil religion has used the Bible selectively in interpreting its responsibility to poorer nations. It has turned mostly to the narratives of God acting in history as the deliverer of his people. This focus fit well with the gratitude of a largely immigrant population for their own deliverance and prosperity, but obscured America's role toward her neighbors. A curious inversion took place as those who had been delivered cast themselves as the "rescuers" of the less fortunate. Stressing God's gracious intervention also led to periodic generosity during disasters but little concern to remedy the enduring structures of injustice. "Emphasis on deliverance after the exodus model," state Birch and Rasmussen, "has led to a great emphasis in the churches on aid and relief as a response to world resource problems, but not enough attention has been given to the restructuring needed in human society."[24] A closer look at the Sinai

covenant indicates the Pentateuch's commitment to provide for the
poor in a structural fashion.

Turning to other literature in the Old Testament, we find new
perspectives to complement that gained from the narratives of God's
intervention. Wisdom literature and the creation accounts present an
appreciation of God's blessings in the very order of our world and
not primarily in his saving acts in history. "To be wise, then, is to
recognize and actualize the potential for full life already inherent in
the created order," the authors write. "To know God is to discern
the harmonious order for which we were created: persons to God;
persons to each other; and persons to the rest of nature. Much of
Wisdom literature is devoted to practical instruction in such discernment."[25] Although at first glance Wisdom literature looks surprisingly secular and irrelevant to a faith-filled morality, it rests on a
recognition of God's presence in the continuing structures of creation. It appreciates the role of human intelligence in creating appropriate actions and institutions without waiting for some authoritative
revelation of God's intentions.

The Genesis material provides another essential corrective to
the deliverance imagery of Exodus. Human beings are created within
and not above nature; they are not self-sufficient rational beings set
over against the rest. Stewardship over creation is a vocation to cher-
ish its goodness. "The commission . . . is to a kind of trusteeship,"
explain Birch and Rasmussen, "not a granting to humanity of inherent power to use as humans themselves see fit."[26] The Eden tragedy
highlights the limits of human capacities. Sin ruptures the relationship with both creation and God; it is a defiant attempt to exercise
unlimited power. When we view redemption in Christ as new creation, we locate human healing within a restored created order in
which human arrogance does not attempt to exploit natural resources as if the rest of creation were exclusively for humanity's benefit.

Historical literature and prophetic eschatology offer additional
perspectives that make our response to justice issues more nuanced.
Prophetic judgment and promise call for responses of both hope and
repentance. They point to a *shalom* of universal reconciliation and a
holistic vision of human flourishing. Any adequate Christology must

have this same expansive definition of human peace as God's intention.

## The Problem of Vanishing Rules

Birch and Rasmussen spell out both the promise and the pitfalls of a perspectival use of Scripture. They argue for a polyphonic approach to biblical imagery in which each strand is complemented by others in a rich blending and harmony. Indictment abstracted from promise betrays the prophet's message; the exercise of human responsibility that ignores its interrelation with the rest of nature is equally unbiblical. The end of their presentation, however, is unsatisfying. Because they concentrate on perspectives and the dispositions of the agent, they ignore the role of moral norms. In each chapter, they suggest different attitudes and approaches to social problems but steadfastly refuse to offer specific moral norms. They thus manifest some of Niebuhr's own reluctance to be specific about action guides. While it seems necessary to place the conversion of the agent at the top of the agenda of Christian ethics, one wonders whether the converted life could use a little more normative clarity. How do we acquire new dispositions except by acting? Could the commands to act in new ways be the beachhead for these new attitudes?

The very shock of the Sermon on the Mount's commands, for example, can be the occasion of a change of heart. I may delude myself in assuming I am being socially generous when, in fact, I am only investing in those who can return the favor. If the Lord commands me to invite unattractive strangers to my dinner parties, then I am caught up short by the bluntness of the order. There are important theological reasons for avoiding legalism. Moral norms, however, may be psychologically necessary and ethically indispensable in a full Christian ethics. Perhaps that is why biblical authors often make the moral demands of the covenant categorically specific. It is one thing to advocate, "Do not resist evil with evil"; it is even more illuminating to prescribe, "Turn the other cheek."

The next approach will stretch our attention in a more concrete direction while attempting to retain the benefits of a perspectival use of Scripture. *Discipleship* implies a more active stance than prophetic discernment. Prophets see and foresee; disciples listen and do the bidding of their master. The Catholic theologian Avery Dulles recently wrote that discipleship provides the most adequate model for describing Christian life in community. It clarifies the difference between Church and world and it emphasizes the personal nature of Christian commitment. It makes very specific demands based on the particular way of life found in the Master.

> The disciple in the New Testament sense is always one who, like Jesus, has been called, and the call is attributed not only to Jesus but also to the Father. The call is an imperious one that overrides all other concerns and obligations, even the need to bury one's own father (Lk 9:59f). The vocation to discipleship means a radical break from the world and its values. In the Synoptic Gospels, especially, we see discipleship as involving a total renunciation of family, property, income, worldly ambition, and even personal safety. The disciple, in the ideal case, forsakes all other security, making a total commitment to Jesus and the Kingdom.[27]

Much that is written under the rubric of discipleship ethics builds upon the important work of H. Richard Niebuhr. It also seeks to remedy the perceived lack of specific moral guidance by turning more directly to the words and example of Jesus as the way of life that concretely guides the Christian.

# 5
# Call to Discipleship

We now move to the most practical use of New Testament material for moral guidance, discipleship that deliberately patterns actions on those of Jesus of Nazareth. Employing the symbols of Scripture challenges the self-understanding of the agent and demands discernment to discover an appropriate response to God acting in our history. Discipleship begins with the conviction that the most appropriate path is the one already blazed by Jesus and that the Christian must creatively embody that way of life in all situations. The moral question, "What ought I to do?" is recast in more particular terms: "How should I act as a disciple of Jesus in these circumstances?" It does not go as far as the devotional classic of the late nineteenth century, *In His Steps,* by Charles M. Sheldon,[1] which posed the question, "What would Jesus do?" The three authors we shall examine take a mediated approach, turning to the story of Jesus, New Testament parables and moral norms to chart the path for the contemporary disciple.

Each of the authors uses slightly different literary material in the New Testament in considering the call to discipleship. Stanley Hauerwas focuses on the distinctive *story* of Jesus, which must become our own guiding story and find its expression in the Christian community. Sallie McFague refines the narrative approach by selecting *parable* as the basic revelatory medium. A parable is an extended metaphor that shocks the reader into new meaning and calls for a response. Finally, John Howard Yoder emphasizes the *normative material* of the New Testament, which must be interpreted through a political reading of the cross of Christ. Although Yoder and other Mennonite Christians do not advocate literal obedience to biblical rules, they do insist that Jesus proclaimed a social ethic that is applicable to the modern world. The three authors concentrate on the New Testament and the particular words and actions of Jesus as God's revelation of a distinctive way of life for believers to follow. None of them makes the error of reducing Jesus to a moral teacher, although this model of discipleship is prone to such a misreading. Jesus proclaimed the beginning of the reign of God and brought about reconciliation with the Father through his life, death and resurrection. His message is primarily one of salvation, not of morality, but the Gospel accounts provide a wealth of details that make him an example to imitate, a model for believers to learn from. A disciple learns from a master and is eager for instruction and faithful response.

## Literary Media and Moral Messages

This chapter also makes the richest purchase on literary forms from the Scriptures. Literary and sociological criticism supplement the traditional forms of biblical criticism, form and redaction criticism. Since the Bible is not only an historical document but also a collection of diverse literary forms of expression, attention to the dynamics of these forms can yield a deeper appreciation of Scripture. In *The Analogical Imagination,* David Tracy argues that the literary media shape the theological messages of biblical revelation.[2] We have seen this same correspondence of medium and message in previous chapters. The authors have selected those forms of expression most congenial to their theological convictions on Christian ethics. Bonhoeffer cited the passages of calling because for him God's word is a command that calls for unhesitating obedience. Niebuhr selected biblical symbols because they are the keys to reinterpreting both self and situation. The Catholic moral theologians selected action-guiding norms grounded on a Christocentric theology of creation. The authors had to select some form from the array of biblical materials, and they justified their choices with theological and moral argument. This pluralism of literary forms and diversity of theologies in the canon prevent just one systematic formulation of biblical ethics.

Birch and Rasmussen showed that certain bodies of Old Testament material, such as Wisdom literature, were overlooked by theologians who stressed God's action in history. Including these neglected literary forms balanced the salvation-history approach with a reminder of God's presence in the structures of creation. Even though the authors selected one literary form as central, they should show how other literature in Scripture is regulated by that main one.

For both Hauerwas and McFague, stories are the key to Christian ethics. In McFague's view, stories claim us because they operate like metaphors on our understanding. In some quarters recently, narrative has become an important theological category. Since most biblical revelation takes the form of a story, first of Israel and then of Jesus, why not examine how a story makes an impact on its hearers? *What* is revealed may be intrinsically connected with *how* it is revealed. H. Richard Niebuhr asked this question forty years ago in *The Meaning of Revelation.*[3] He argued that conversion occurred when a new self-understanding arose, a reinterpretation of one's own history in light of the revelation of God. Each of us seeks a unified context to make sense out of the disparate events of our lives. Without that context, we are only fragmented selves, moral chameleons who are creatures of the diverse environments we inhabit. The unity we need for a sense of continuity and integrity cannot come from an idea or a system of thought. It must be a "dramatic unity," a process in which personal unity unfolds gradually over time. In a word, what we need is a "story" with a beginning, a middle and an end that can help the self grasp its origin and destiny. How else do we gradually disclose ourselves to new friends but by recounting our own story in countless memories and anecdotes?

Stories also embody certain characteristic ways of acting; they shape our behavior as well as report it. The story implicit in the life of a Trappist monk like Thomas Merton indicates different choices than the story of the ambitious MBA plunging into corporate America. Answering the question, "What story do I choose to embody?" reveals both my uniqueness as well as directions I can expect to take. Appropriately, God's revelation takes the form of story because only that medium can communicate God's personal reality and challenge the self-understanding of the story's hearers. When we join a community, we adopt its story as our own, recasting our significant memories and aspirations in accord with this story. As a result, we have a different story to "confess." George Stroup writes, "The confessional narratives of Christian believers are the result of the collision between the faith narratives of the Christian community and the believer's personal history. To confess faith in Jesus Christ is to reconstruct that personal identity narrative in light of the community's *Credo*."[4] Discipleship ethics cites the specific story of Jesus as the challenging norm for the new self-understanding and action of his followers. It does not disguise the conflict between that story and the dominant stories of our world.

## I.  Hauerwas: The Story of Faith

Stanley Hauerwas uses story as the key to interpreting Scripture to outline the path of Christian discipleship. He fuses some of the best contributions of Protestant and Roman Catholic ethics to argue for a distinctive transformation of character that serves as the center of this discipleship. By his own description, he is "a Methodist of doubtful theological background . . . who teaches and worships with and is sustained morally and financially by Roman Catholics, who believes that the most nearly faithful form of Christian witness is best exemplified by the often unjustly ignored people called Anabaptists or Mennonites."[5]

Hauerwas has taught for several years at the University of Notre Dame where his colleague, John Howard Yoder, has been a strong influence on him. Early in his writings, Hauerwas developed an ethics of character that stressed the gradual self-formation of the moral agent, which is often overlooked by moral philosophers who concentrate on decisions and the norms that guide them. Dissatisfied with Barth and Bultmann for ignoring the integrity and continuity that lend shape to our characters, Hauerwas found in Aristotle and Aquinas an account of how the virtues give consistency to the self. We are not people whose morality emerges at occasional moments of decision, but people with a gradually developing consistency that places those decisions in a personal context. We expect an honest person's concern for truth and candor to be consistent, not just a fleeting effort to keep promises that may be difficult to fulfill. The

Christian life is more than a series of existential decisions or moments of obedience to a clear command of God.

Neither Aquinas nor Aristotle could describe the particular virtues that should shape the character of Christians; rather, they spoke in general terms of human virtues that could apply to anyone. Hauerwas uncovered the normative virtues for Christians in the story of Jesus presented by the Gospels. Essential to consistent character is a *way of life,* a concrete pattern of expectations that guides commitments. Christians are shown their way of life in the story of Jesus and are called to follow his way faithfully. Such fidelity both shapes the characters of individuals and produces the distinctive community called the Church. Hauerwas derived the notion of story from H. Richard Niebuhr, but he departs from Niebuhr on three points. First, the Gospel narrative presents a more specific call than the exploratory discernment that uses biblical symbols to interpret events. Second, Hauerwas corrects Niebuhr's "intuitionism" by presenting a normative pattern of conscious virtuous dispositions. Third, he insists that the Church must be the location for reflecting on what God is doing in one's life.

Hauerwas succinctly states that the use of Scripture is as a call to discipleship. He writes, "The moral use of Scripture, therefore, lies precisely in its power to help us remember the story of God for the continual guidance of our community and individual lives."[6] The three foundations of his argument are: (a) the narrative, which shapes Christian life, (b) the community of the Church as the place where Scripture has authority, and (c) the inadequacy of more philosophical accounts of Christian ethics. We will look at each of these in turn and then test the theory with two narratives, Augustine's *Confessions* and Albert Speer's *Inside the Third Reich,* to contrast a truthful narrative with a self-deceptive one.

## *The Story Defines the Disciple*

The Gospel of Mark focuses on the collision between Peter's understanding of the Christian way of life and that of Jesus. It shows how story defines discipleship. In Mk 8:27—9:1, Peter first acknowledges that Jesus is the Christ and then immediately rejects Jesus' description of the way of suffering and death that lies ahead. "Jesus thus rebukes Peter," writes Hauerwas, "who had learned the name but not the story that determines the meaning of the name."[7] Peter had a different story for the title "the Christ," who was in his mind the victorious Messiah who would restore the power and glory of Israel. Jesus spells out the implications of his own way: it must become the way of the disciples as well. "If anyone would come after me let him deny himself and take up his cross and follow me. For whoever would save his life will lose it; and whoever loses his life for my sake and the Gospel's will save it. For what does it profit anyone to gain the whole world and forfeit his life" (Mk 8:34-36)?

The story of the impending disgrace of Jesus is not one to be taken lightly or an anecdote to be glossed over. It challenges the truth of Peter's existence and exposes the falsity of his ambitions. Either this story changes Peter and the other hearers so that they embark on that fateful journey, or else they cease to be Jesus' disciples. Note the story's concreteness. It cannot be resolved into a general teaching on self-sacrifice or an abstract ethical theory on the difficulty of the virtuous life. The message is inseparable from the person of Jesus. "Just as truth is not freeing unless it is his truth," writes Hauerwas, "so sacrifice will not help us unless it is the sacrifice that is done in the name and form of the Kingdom as we find it in his life. There is no truth beyond him: his story is the truth of the Kingdom. And that truth turns out to be the cross."[8] We cannot learn the truth of the Kingdom without following the way of Jesus; his story defines God's way of ruling, which is paradoxically bound to the cross.

For Hauerwas, like Niebuhr, Christian ethics aims to transform the self-understanding of the agent. Here the dominant story that shapes the character of the would-be disciple clashes with the story of Jesus. All the costly sayings of the Gospels reinforce this collision of a worldly way of life and discipleship. They disturb us because they assault our complacent self-understanding, which would like the Gospel to co-exist peacefully with the way of the world. The messianic expectations of Peter were a "counter-story" to the way of life embodied in Jesus. That is why Jesus had to confront it directly. What we do and how we do it are ultimately rooted in a way of life, a story that shapes our self-understanding and that of the communities to which we belong. No one can have a completely private story: a way of life is always determined by a specific community to which we are loyal. We learn how to be virtuous by the example of others in the community; their witness inspires us to be virtuous. This story shapes a community capable of ordering its existence in a manner appropriate to this story. For Christians that community is the Church. Every way of life has its own story; what is distinctive about Christians' community is the story of Jesus of Nazareth.

## The Story Defines the Community

How do we deal with practical matters with this theory? Discipleship is not translatable into a slate of rules or pre-determined moral responses. *How* we act is even more important than *what* we do. The way of life inculcates certain virtues, skills that help the community navigate the new reality envisioned by the story. We measure a person's character by virtues, by the moral readiness and dispositions that shape conduct. In addition, only the virtuous person takes responsibility for his or her character; virtues give the character self-possession and integrity. No consensus exists among philosophers on what the proper virtues are for human life because each different culture and historical era has a limited purchase on human experience. Virtues are context-dependent as well as narrative-dependent.

An adequate and effective community story encourages its adherents to face the particular challenges and tragedies of life. Christians, however, believe the story of Jesus not because of its functional value in ordering life but because of its truthfulness. Because no all-encompassing theory of virtues exists apart from a tradition, no abstract evaluation of a way of life can be made prior to adopting it. At this level, only a practical test is possible: What kind of people does this community and its story produce? The life of the Church is the acid test of the truthfulness of its story. It must live up to its proclamation or it gives the lie to the Gospel. If virtues can be learned only by observing and imitating the virtuous, then discipleship depends upon saints.

The primary social task of the Church is to be itself authentically. It may challenge secular society on specific issues, but it must first be visibly different from the world. It must identify the various counter-stories of the culture, which render characters incompatible with the story of Jesus. The great unacknowledged story of our liberal democracy is that of the autonomous agent who lives according to self-interest, enters only contractual relationships and values maximum range of freedom above all. At best, this is the story of Gary Cooper in "High Noon," the loner sheriff fighting for justice; at worst, it is the violent world of the cowboys and police-mavericks portrayed by Clint Eastwood.

Discipleship redefines the standards of morality in a distinctively Christian direction by locating them within the guiding story of the tradition. For example, the biblical prohibition of adultery cannot be abstracted from the meaning of marriage that is possible in Jewish and Christian communities. The commandment against adultery does not rest on philosophical convictions about the legitimate expression of sexuality, but on this view of marriage. "Marriage in those communities," writes Hauerwas, "derives from profound hope in and commitment to the future, witnessed by the willingness and duty to bring new life into the world. Moreover for those traditions family and marriage have special significance as they are also an expression of the relation these people have with their God."[9] The Church should serve as witness to the world by unmasking the secular story of marriage as romantic. Rather than simply repeat the biblical prohibition of divorce, it should provide a counter-story rooted in Christian sacrifice, which can often be heroic.

Virtues like hope and patience undergo a similar redefinition. Hope sustains every virtue because it gives us confidence that the moral life is worth the effort, that it is an adventure worth taking. It needs to be tempered by patience, the virtue that enables us to persevere when results are not forthcoming. "Without denying that there may be non-religious accounts of hope and patience," states Hauerwas, "Jews and Christians have been the people that have stressed the particular importance of these virtues. For they are the people formed by the conviction that our existence is bounded by a power that is good and faithful. Moreover, they are peoples with a deep stake in history. . . ."[10]

In discussing such issues as family and medical ethics, Hauerwas always brings the issue back to the Church. How will the community respond to these issues? He rarely prescribes specific actions. Instead, he attempts to locate these moral problems in the story of Jesus and interpret them in light of that distinctive way of life (without ever exactly defining what it is). Whether this severs Christians from dialogue with those in society who do not share their story is debatable, as evidenced by Hauerwas' disagreement with Catholic moral theologians on abortion.

## Testing the Story's Truth

Hauerwas criticizes any Christian ethics that rests on philosophical systems prescinding from the historical context of a way of life. Natural law thinkers who see in Scripture only a moral reminder of human obligations depend on a common humanity that cuts across historical limits. For Hauerwas, natural law at best negatively limits action: it cannot tell us what to do, even though it may indicate something that is inappropriate for our humanity. Previous natural law formulations accepted as "natural" certain practices which we now see were bound to a particular culture, such as slavery or the subordination of women. They were natural only to those who shared that limited cultural story. The more common account of ethics today is derived from Kantian universalism, which attempts to transcend cultural differences by appealing to a common rationality. It embodies a story that is largely unrecognized: the story of self-sufficient free agents who deal with each other as strangers, not as members of communities with committed roles. The lawsuit rather than the family discussion becomes the paradigm for settling differences. Such formal systems can neither help us judge between stories nor empower us to form a definite character. "For morally there is no neutral story that insures the truthfulness of our particular stories," states Hauerwas. "Moreover, any ethical theory that is sufficiently abstract and universal to claim neutrality would not be able to form character."[11] Although one can agree with this insight into moral particularity, it is unclear whether accepting the insight commits one to the same relativism that Hauerwas at times adopts. Surely there is some resemblance between virtues in various cultures, and we feel justified in criticizing other cultures for practices that may fit their cultural self-understanding but are abhorrent to humanity.

We need to look to specific persons to weight the value of competing stories, because, as Hauerwas says, "the test of each story is the sort of person it shapes."[12] Hauerwas contrasts the classic account of Christian conversion, Augustine's *Confessions,* with the autobiography of Albert Speer, Hitler's chief architect. Just as H.

Richard Niebuhr wrote that "evil imaginations of the heart" obscured the truth of our lives, certain stories are exercises in self-deception. They systematically blind us to unpleasant contradictions between action and self-understanding.

In his search for understanding, the young Augustine embraced two communities and their corresponding stories but found both of them inadequate. The Manichees divorced evil from God by describing a cosmic dualism. Augustine realized, however, that if human immorality resulted from a mixture of the two cosmic principles in the individual, human responsibility would be a fiction. The Platonists believed that both God and the human soul were based on innate light and power. Unfortunately, this story rested on formal notions that were powerless to set Augustine's heart aright. Hauerwas summarizes the conflict that is recounted in Augustine's *Confessions:*

> His life, however, was framed by facts of another kind: of rights and wrongs dealt to others (6:15); of an order to which he now aspired to conform, but which he found himself unable to accomplish (8:11). . . . He can read [in the Platonists' book] "of the Word, God . . . but not read in them that "the Word was made flesh and came to dwell among us" (Jn 1:14).[13]

Augustine discovered that only the Gospel had the power to transform his life. It did not attempt to explain the inexplicable, the nature of evil, nor did it provide a theory of God that could enable one to conceive the divinity. The *Confessions* show that the answer to these questions is not so much formulated as received. The Word becomes enfleshed in Augustine's own life as God's gracious self-disclosure brings his disciple's struggle to an end.

Albert Speer, on the other hand, in his autobiography *Inside the Third Reich,* provides an example of a story that not only failed to transform but fostered self-deception. Speer was a brilliant young architect from an apolitical family, a cultured and humane individual who nevertheless became Hitler's chief architect and minister of armaments. He ignored rumors of Auschwitz and allowed the use of slave labor. Because he did not consider himself anti-semitic, he felt no personal responsibility for the persecution of the Jews. "I felt myself to be Hitler's architect," he wrote. "Political events did not concern me."[14]

Speer wanted to use his profession as the sole source of meaning in his life and let the story of the apolitical technician function as the narrative for his character. It was an inadequate story, however, because it failed to provide Speer with the necessary skills to limit that role and confront the truth of what his work was actually accomplishing. Hauerwas writes, "His self-deception began when he assumed that 'being above all an architect' was a story sufficient to constitute his self."[15] In Nuremberg years later, where he was imprisoned for his complicity in the Reich, he was disturbed by the ease with which he had so totally assumed this identity. He wrote, "I did not see any moral ground outside the system where I should have taken my stand."[16]

Hauerwas insists that many similar stories can promote such self-deception. A truthful story exposes the tragedy and compromising nature of our lives. Only the story of Jesus, which asserts the necessity of the cross, can shape a self capable of facing such unpleasant truths. Discipleship will always go against the grain. "If the true God were to provide us with a saving story," writes Hauerwas, "it would have to be one that we found continually discomforting."[17] Much of his writing seems devoted to unmasking the dominant but unacknowledged stories our culture provides for personal identity. This enterprise is limited by the brevity with which he articulates the practical consequences of the story of Jesus. He might reply that we should go to the Church rather than to theologians for this moral guidance.

Although Hauerwas convincingly argues that we must calibrate our own way of life to the particular contours of the story of Jesus, he does not explain precisely how the literary impact of a story effects human transformation. We listen to many stories for amusement or curiosity, stories that do not call for radical change in our lives. How does the New Testament story make such a claim on us?

## II.   McFague: Speaking in Parables

Sallie McFague addresses the moral dynamics of story in her book, *Speaking in Parables*. She employs literary analysis to examine

several of the forms found in the Bible. For her, the message of
Scripture is coordinate with that central expression of the teaching of
Jesus, the parable. Because these concrete vignettes jar us out of a
familiar world into one with new, compelling possibilities, states
McFague, "parables are for bringing people to commitment."[18] Since
parables are extended metaphors, the dynamics of parable rest on the
power of metaphor. They serve as "food for thought," an expression
that stretches our imaginations because it juxtaposes an unfamiliar
pair of words; as we digest metaphors they function as nourishment
for meaning. The Gospel generates its meaning in this indirect fashion by placing the familiar in an unfamiliar context. We realize the
impact of metaphor not by grasping a literal statement but by
moving through the metaphor to new meaning. "If we say," writes
McFague, "as I would want to, that Jesus of Nazareth is par excel-
lence the metaphor of God, we mean that his familiar, mundane story is the *way,* the indirect but necessary way, from here to there. . . .
Metaphoric meaning is a *process,* not a momentary, static insight: it
operates like a story, moving from here to there, from 'what is' to
'what might be.' "[19]

Let us consider a simple parable of the Kingdom. In Matthew
13, Jesus states: "The Kingdom of heaven is like a merchant's search
for fine pearls. When he found one really valuable pearl, he went
back and put up for sale all that he had and bought it" (vv. 45–46).
If I take this expression literally, I miss the point. I have to enter
imaginatively into this mini-story and participate in its movement. I
can understand how a shrewd merchant would take a plunge like
this, sell everything and borrow whatever he needed to acquire the
one pearl that could make his fortune.

This parable can be a dangerous experiment if I get caught up in
its logic: it states indirectly that the Kingdom of God is priceless, but
can only be attained by spending all that I have upon it. Upon reach-
ing such a conclusion, I am no longer interpreting the parable; it is
interpreting me. It leads me to commitment by exposing my lack of
commitment. Being a disciple of Jesus is an important value in my
life, but not my only allegiance. I have some "side bets" out just in
case, a diversified portfolio for my investments. Granted, it makes
sense for this merchant who is sure about the pearl to take such a

serious risk for it. Does my hedging mean that I don't estimate the Kingdom so highly? Or does it expose a fatal cowardice? Without selling everything, that pearl would elude the merchant. Is it the same with me and the Kingdom? These two verses of Scripture which seemed so innocuous before become utterly demanding if I enter into the metaphor and let it shock me into new awareness of my own compromises, which are unmasked as cowardice and stupidity. It is no wonder that Jesus irritated so many of his hearers. On the other hand, the parable is good news, too. It moves me from what is to what might be: if that merchant could muster the courage to lose all in order to gain all, might I not be able to do the same?

Parables are destroyed by moralizing. If I try to avoid the imaginative involvement in the parable by reducing it to a "moral," my life remains unchanged. Parables hold "in solution" belief, language and the life to which we are called.[20] Abstracting a moral from a parable would be like boiling off the solution to produce a distillate. Take as an example the parable of the unmerciful servant who throttles his fellow servant over a trifling debt after he himself had just been forgiven a staggering amount by his lord. The logic of mercy dramatically exposes the logic of vengeance, and the unforgiving servant loses his master's forgiveness by his own callousness toward his fellow (Mt 81:21-35). Jesus tells this parable in response to Peter's question, "Lord, when my brother wrongs me, how often must I forgive him?" The parable tells us more about God's capacity for mercy and our own for vengeance than the simple answer, "seventy times seven." We are called to endless forgiveness because we have been forgiven so much by God. Hence, the parable empowers such forgiveness by appealing to memory and imagination and not merely to moral logic. Moralizing is the work of the spectator who prefers to keep a distance from the shock of the parable, which demands that the listener participate in its message and embody its truth in practice.

*Jesus the Incarnate Parable*

The story of Jesus, then, is an extended parable because it concretely embodies the shocking love of God. It places our familiar compromises and mundane expectations in a new context, empowering us to move from compromise to commitment. Parable is the literary expression most appropriate for a religion founded on incarnation, the embodiment of infinite graciousness in a concrete life. Parable is the key to interpreting the rest of the story of Jesus. McFague writes, "The gospels and parables are not histories but re-enactments of good news—dramatic narratives that 'say' the same thing that the big story, the story of Jesus' passion, death, and resurrection says."[21]

I would say that parables present the presuppositions of New Testament morality rather than constitute that morality itself. They expose our distance from the Kingdom and God's willingness to bridge that distance. As such, they are the flash points of revelation, the literary form through which the Kingdom's logic bursts into our lives. Parables, however, need to be supplemented by symbol, command, doctrine and the other resources found in Scripture. When Paul wrestles with the pastoral problems of his congregations, he constantly gravitates toward the central metaphor for the Christian journey, the cross and resurrection of Jesus, but he still employs an entire arsenal of moral equipment, from analogy to moral norms, to specify practical Christian conduct.

The life of the disciple must be defined by the life of the master. The authors of this approach to Scripture, more than any others, keep our attention closely fixed on the actual life of Jesus of Nazareth. To journey with him is to repudiate our former way of life and accept the paradoxical goal of that journey, the cross. McFague uses metaphor as the trigger of conversion, the shocking juxtaposition of meaning that can empower the decision to become a disciple of Jesus. She strives to restore the offensive quality of the parables, which we have become oblivious to from hearing them so often. Hauerwas sheds more light on the dynamics of life after conversion when the story of Jesus needs to provide some continuity to our values and conduct. As interpreted by the Church, the way of life present in the Gospel is translated into the virtues that serve as skills to negotiate Christian life in a world that decidedly does not share the Gospel story. Neither Hauerwas nor McFague devotes much attention to moral norms and principles to guide Christian practice for the disciple.

### III. John Howard Yoder: The New Law of Christ

John Howard Yoder complements their treatments by concentrating on the specific commands of Jesus found in the New Testament. Do the Gospels present a social ethic? Most critics would be reluctant to respond affirmatively, but Yoder discovers a definite social ethics in the New Testament. If we can suspend our usual presumption that the concrete prescriptions of Jesus or Paul were only for their specific culture at that time, we find a definite program for discipleship in political action. In *The Politics of Jesus,* Yoder examines the Gospel of Luke and finds in the ministry of Jesus a specific challenge to the existing authorities. Once this political option is unearthed, it opens up many other parts of the New Testament, from Paul to Revelation. It also steers Christian reflection away from secular forms of moral wisdom back to the person of Jesus. Yoder writes, "The substitution of nature or history for Jesus as the locus of revelation was justified by the claim that Jesus had nothing to say on this subject. . . . But now we see that he did have something to say; in fact that he said little that was not somehow on this subject."[22]

The events of Luke's Gospel show that Jesus confronted a difficult political option, rejecting both the quietist retreat from responsibility of the Essenes and the crusading resort to violence of the Zealots. He chose instead to resist the established powers of his time by non-violent means, inaugurating a new way of life that would eventually threaten them and cost his own life. Disciples are called to imitate Jesus only at this point: to resist the established powers resolutely, but without resorting to the weapons of the old order. "The believer's cross," writes Yoder, "is no longer any and every kind of suffering, sickness, or tension, the bearing of which is demanded. The believer's cross must be, like his Lord's, the price of his social non-conformity . . . it is the end of a path freely chosen after counting the cost."[23] The specific norms of the Sermon on the Mount are therefore not impossible ideals nor spiritual counsels: "turning the other cheek" and "walking the extra mile" are spoken literally to the disciple. The will of God is not determined by historical circumstances, which can relativize these awkward prescriptions. Rather, as Yoder says, "the will of God is affirmatively, concretely knowable in the person and ministry of Jesus."[24] If the Church of disciples takes the same journey as the Master, it can expect the same resistance from the forces of oppression that killed him.

When we read the rest of the New Testament through this interpretation of the non-violent cross, several prescriptive passages take on an unsuspected relevance. Yoder takes such prescriptive material as Romans 13:1–6 and the "household codes" (e.g., Col 3:18—4:1) and reverses the traditionally conservative readings that seem to mandate apolitical submission. He finds them to be instances of "revolutionary subordination," which does not rule out conscientious resistance on the part of the subordinate party.

Finally, the cross of Christ calls into question one of our era's most cherished social assumptions, namely, that we are in control of history and responsible for getting it to turn out right. Yoder states that the politics of Jesus asks us to be faithful rather than effective: the positive results are in God's hands, not ours. Our fundamental categories for conceiving political responsibility must be recast. "The relationship between the obedience of God's people," writes Yoder, "and the triumph of God's cause is not a relationship of cause and effect but one of cross and resurrection."[25] Non-violent resistance in imitation of Jesus is not a technique to control history or society; the cross is no recipe for resurrection. The vindication is God's affair; fidelity to the inevitable cross must be the sole concern of the Christian community. The history of the Mennonites as an active and persecuted prophetic minority lends authenticity to this demanding position.

For each of the authors we have studied in this chapter, Scripture issues a call to discipleship. The Christian finds a new pattern for morality in the shape of the life of Jesus of Nazareth. Neither the secular culture nor general human experience provides insight into the life of discipleship unless scrutinized in terms of the particular values found in the Gospel. The incarnation is not an endorsement of all that is humanly good but a radical break with the fallen condition of humanity. While other theologians find Scripture to be a moral reminder of behavior that is already consonant with our humanity, this approach could never accept the reduction of Christian ethics to the message "Be human." Christians are called to be human in a specific way, in close imitation of their Master. The central event of his life was the paradoxical tragedy of the cross, "a stumbling block to Jews and an absurdity to Gentiles" (1 Cor 1:23). Both Hauerwas and Yoder stress that the Church's way of living should always be out of step with the dominant culture.

Is this fundamentalism? I do not believe that charge can be fairly made against these authors. They do not attempt to find an answer to every modern problem in isolated verses of Scripture. They are explicit about their theological interpretation and the selection of material. Hauerwas sketches a theory of the moral agent, of character and virtues. McFague carefully defines the role of metaphor and story in human decision and insight. Yoder shifts from the moral agent to the moral act, arguing that many of the actual commands of the New Testament have a social application in our culture, even while they contradict some of that culture's basic assumptions.

# 6
# Scripture as Basis for Responding Love

This chapter will present what I believe is the most adequate and comprehensive approach for using Scripture in ethics. It answers the moral question, "What ought I to do?" by finding the motive and the norm for loving others in the witness of God's love in Scripture that has been confirmed in the agent's experience. Love is the norm and the central motivation in New Testament ethics; because it is initiated by God, it always has the character of response.

The love which is the central norm for the Christian life is not an abstract principle but a specific type of experience. It is the experience of God's distinctive way of loving as manifested in the history of Jesus Christ and continued through his Spirit in the believing community. How can an experience or an individual history be normative for a way of life? Like many theological ethicians, Yoder selects a particular central aspect of that history and makes it normative for Jesus' disciples: only the non-violent cross of political resistance is held up for imitation by subsequent generations of Christians. Other theologians move further back from the life of Jesus to select a dominant characteristic, such as self-sacrificial love, as the determining guide for Christian ethics. One must acknowledge, however, some danger in selecting either a central event or moral value to stand for the richness of an historical existence, of a complex person such as the Gospels present Jesus to be.

We must find a way to permit the richness of the person of Christ to serve as the guiding norm for Christian experience and moral practice. The previous two chapters held up dominant biblical symbols and the narrative of salvation as normative for Christians. In this chapter we will add a distinctive set of Christian affections to symbol and narrative. Christian experience is shaped by a set of symbols on one side and a set of affections on the other. It is accountable to them both, because biblical symbols and affections present the distinctive way of loving to which Christian life is a response. The right and good moral action for the Christian is the one that is the appropriate concrete response to this experience of being loved by God in Christ.

This approach focuses on the change of "heart" and the dynamics that dispose the heart to action, the *affections*. Jeremiah and Ezekiel described the new covenant as a radical change of the heart through a new personal awareness of God and his guidance, a replacement of the unresponsive stony hearts with hearts of flesh.[1] Although no single verse can capture the rich diversity of the moral teachings of Scripture, the principle enunciated by Jesus in John 13:34 is perhaps the most comprehensive. We are commanded to love one another in just the same way that Jesus has loved us. Because Scripture's witness of that love shapes the heart and its affections, it functions as a "school of the affections." We will concentrate on the Johannine and Pauline writings, psalms and doxology, and prophetic lyric poetry, even though every literary form in the canon helps shape the affections that are central to moral life.

Theologians who have interpreted Scripture in this manner range from the Old Testament scholar Gerhard von Rad to James M. Gustafson.[2] The argument advanced here will seek support from them but is more of a personal synthesis than are the other chapters of this book. Let us summarize the argument at the outset. The affections are the central dispositions of moral character that lead to particular ways of acting. Affections are defined by the experiences that give rise to them and by the objects toward which they tend. Scripture both evokes and directs the affections in distinctive ways. Therefore, biblical symbols and narratives have a normative correlation with a distinctive set of affections that form Christian character in community.

## The New Commandment of Jesus

Before developing the origins and objects of Christian affectivity, let us turn to the specific context of the new commandment of Jesus in order to examine the dynamics which school the affections. The narrative of the foot-washing acts out as a parable the meaning of this distinctive new command. Note that this new principle is not the two great commandments of the Synoptics or the oft-cited version of the golden rule, "Do unto others as you would have them do unto you." Instead it reads in the New American Bible translation, "I give you a new commandment: Love one another. Such as my love has been for you, so must your love be for each other. This is how all will know you for my disciples: your love for one another" (13:34–35). The love they have experienced from Jesus should be both the norm and the motivation for their love of others. Their love continues the mission of Jesus' life by being sent to witness to others. Memory and intention define this command by reference to the specific history of Jesus.

Jesus' words conclude his shocking symbolic action of taking the role of a slave to wash the disciples' feet. John 13 is the transition from what Raymond E. Brown has called the Book of Signs (the public ministry) to the Book of Glory (the climactic sign that will reveal his glory when he is lifted up on the cross).[3] This scene may serve as prologue to the Book of Glory as the Logos hymn did to the whole Gospel. Theologically, this enacted parable seems to have a eucharistic reference. There is no institutional narrative in John's account of the Last Supper. This parable embodies the moral significance of the eucharistic discourse of John 6 as it demonstrates the moral implications of communion in the body of Christ.

The scene opens on a mixture of affective qualities—love and betrayal, lofty mission and impending humiliation—that intensifies the symbolic weight of the action that follows:

Before the feast of Passover, Jesus realized that the hour had come for him to pass from this world to the Father. He had loved his own in this world, and would show his love for them to the end. The devil had already induced Judas,

son of Simon Iscariot, to hand him over; and so, during the
supper, Jesus—fully aware that he had come from God and
was going to God, the Father who had handed everything
over to him—rose from the meal and took off his cloak. He
picked up a towel and tied it around himself. Then he
poured water into a basin and began to wash his disciples'
feet and dry them with the towel he had around him
(13:1–5).

This paradoxical action, so puzzling to the recipients, defines his love
for them and the significance of the tragic events that were about to
unfold. Placed at this pivotal position in the structure of John, the
washing of the feet interprets both the public ministry and the passion. The disciples must allow Jesus to perform this service; Peter's
embarrassment cannot exempt him from it. Once they have been
served by Jesus their own lives are irrevocably implicated. "But if I
washed your feet—I who am Teacher and Lord—then you must
wash each other's feet. What I just did was to give you an example:
as I have done, so you must do. I solemnly assure you, no slave is
greater than his master . . ." (13:14–16). But if the master has become a slave for you, that must become normative for your action
toward others.

The new commandment goes beyond *imitation* to *participation*.
Certainly the disciples do not understand the mandate as a demand
for external copying. Eucharist, not foot-washing, becomes the central commemorative ritual of the post-resurrection community.
Rather, their service evolves out of participation in the life of Christ
as they enter into the same humiliation and exaltation he underwent.
They are called to embody a particular life which now vivifies them
through the gift of the Spirit, organically connecting them to Jesus as
branches to a vine (Jn 15). They are not called to embody an abstract
principle or a set of values, but a distinctive existence. If there is conscious imitation, it will stem from this participation and emerge from
within in response to the Spirit that conforms the disciple's life to
that of the Master. They are empowered to live a new way of life by
the Spirit which dwells within them and their community.

**The Life of Jesus and Our Way of Life**

The new commandment has bedeviled systematic theologians because it refers not to a concept but to an entire way of life or, more specifically, an actual historical life. Its norm is the entire experience of being loved by Jesus, which is parabolically expressed in this foot-washing. In the fifteenth chapter, John comes closer to summarizing its normative content, but once again refers to an historical action: "This is my commandment: love one another as I have loved you. There is no greater love than this: to lay down one's life for one's friends" (15:12–13). In a double sense it is Jesus' own commandment because *he* enunciates it and it is intelligible only in reference to *his* personal history. Norm and motive are inextricably related to each other by being derived from his person. The gratitude evoked by such love impels one to treat others in similar fashion. In this way, the distinctive *agape* that is the life of Jesus is continued. Systematic thinkers who interpret his new command as an instance of some general moral principle are doomed to miss this command's distinctiveness because they prescind from the very narrative that defines the imperative and guides the motive.

We have already mentioned two authors who interpret this love and the affections that express it. H. Richard Niebuhr's Kantian use of symbols which organize affections and Bruno Schüller's theory of Jesus' exemplar causality both contain some insight, but I believe they are ultimately inadequate. Schüller separates motive from content in biblical morality. For him many passages dealing with moral material are in an exhortatory mode because the Gospel encourages us to do what we already know we should do. Norms and values have "truth-value" independent of the Gospel. Christ's action is an example for us but it does not redefine moral meaning. "In fact," writes Schüller, "the exemplarity of God and the exemplarity of Christ are not the standard for the *meaning* of 'to be morally good' but for the *exercise* of moral goodness."[4] Human nature establishes the content for any moral norm or value, and Jesus' example encourages us to be faithful to our own humanity. This seems too severe a separation of motive and content. *Why* we act morally enters into the meaning of *what* we do. Is not the life of Jesus a revelation of a "way" which would not otherwise have been self-evident to unaided human nature? If God has loved us in a forgiving and renewing manner which changes our previous conception of love, should we not be impelled to love others in a qualitatively new way?

H. Richard Niebuhr explains motive and meaning in affectivity with a more Kantian analysis. In objective reasoning our ideas help order the confusing swarm of sense data into more intelligible patterns. "By means of ideas we interpret as we sense, and sense as we interpret."[5] Imagination uses pertinent symbols and images to decipher the conflicting possibilities presented by our senses. These images are usually mechanical or mathematical in objective thought. In the personal realm, we use images of persons to order the brute data of our affections. "We meet each one," says Niebuhr, "with an imagination whereby we supply what is lacking in the immediate datum and are enabled to respond, rightly or wrongly, to a whole of reality of which this affection is for us a symbol and a part."[6] Christians use the life of Jesus Christ as a key image to organize and interpret the affections. As we saw, the crucifixion becomes the ordering image for the confusing welter of pity, horror and outrage caused by the suffering of the innocent in war. This image elicits a different response than viewing the matter through the lens of retributive justice.

Although Niebuhr comes closer than Schüller to integrating motive and content, his theory is still unsatisfactory. The affections seem to be more than mere "brute data" to be shaped by symbolic interpretation. Do they have some intelligibility inherent in them that makes some images more appropriate than others? Does human suffering, for example, contain in some obscure way the paradox of the cross and resurrection so that the explicit symbols reveal what was actually occurring in the suffering? Neither Schüller nor Niebuhr seems to find much intelligibility in the affections themselves. We need a more integrated account of moral meaning and motive to understand the new commandment of Jesus. Examining affections through the originating experiences and their objects may help us grasp the defining role Scripture plays in them.

## I. The Object of Affection

"True religion, in great part, consists in holy affections," wrote the great Puritan theologian Jonathan Edwards in his 1746 work *Re-*

*ligious Affections.*[7] This principle offers the most promising avenue for investigating the role of Scripture in moral life. If Christian experience is rooted in the affections, we should expect Christianity's charter document to be addressed in large part to them. Affections are the basic motivations that shape an individual's character; they are also dispositions for acting in ways consonant with a person's convictions and commitments. Affections are both stable and dynamic aspects of the character because they deepen if they are acted out, fade if they are ignored. More permanent facets of motivation than feeling and under more control than moods, affections continue to exist in the agent even when not being experienced consciously. An older vocabulary referred to them as habits of the soul, virtues and vices that lead to specific ways of evaluating and acting.

One useful way to examine the affections is to look at their origin and their object. Affections are not irrational; rather, they provide a felt, wholistic evaluation of the situation as they grasp its qualitative tone in a way that pure reason could never do. They are sound if object and origin are both properly grounded. For example, fear is a rational reaction to a situation that is objectively threatening. Apprehension, caution and wariness are valid appreciative reactions in certain settings. A late night stroll in a dangerous neighborhood should evoke a sense of danger; only the naive or foolhardy would fail to be wary. On the other hand, when the object is fabricated by the person's fancy, the affection is groundless and inaccurate. The paranoid person generates fear spontaneously and constructs a world of conspiracy out of that fear.

As C.S. Lewis writes, "a desire is turned not to itself but to its object. Not only that, but it owes all its character to its object. Erotic love is not like desire for food, nay, a love for one woman differs from a love for another woman in the very same way and the very same degree as the two women differ from each other. . . . The form of the desired is in the desire."[8] I would only qualify this by adding that the experiences that originate the desire also modify it, but perhaps not so radically as does its object. If both ingredients of desire, or any other affection, are distinctively fashioned by biblical imagery, then the affections will themselves be distinctive.

The object and origin of Christian love define its character. It is not self-generated but responsive to One who has first shown love to the undeserving subject. Both origin and object are personal. Only persons evoke love, and love seeks some sort of union with the beloved. *Agape* is not limited to others who are attractive, which would betray the merciful graciousness that occasioned it originally. It can be commanded, therefore; one does not merely wait to be won over by the goodness or beauty of the other. Christian love is an attitude that becomes a policy as it takes the initiative to aid those in need and to find ways of appreciating them. John 13:34 defines this love by indicating its distinctive origin and object. Because they have been loved by Jesus in a distinctive way, the disciples are empowered and required to love others in this same way. Ultimately, this affection intends to participate in the mission of Jesus by moving those who witness this love to refer back to its origin: "This is how all will know you for my disciples: your love for one another" (13:35). A particular motivation and intention, origin and object thus define Christian *agape*.

## How Scripture Schools the Affections

Scripture schools the affections by presenting the various names the believer uses to address God and the narrative that orders those images into a remembered whole. In religious experience, God is the object of address long before being the object of speculation. We cannot address God under a specific aspect or image unless we assume the affective stance connoted in that image. By revealing the appropriate names of God, Scripture instructs our hearts in new ways of relating to God. Consider what Jesus tells the disciples when they ask him to teach them to pray as John had taught his own followers. He invites them to address God with the same term he uses, as their "Abba" (Lk 11:1–4). This is the revolutionary origin of Christian prayer. This simple name reveals both who God is for them and who they are in relation to him. Because God is the absolute object of love, the first great commandment is appropriate. They are to love this unlimited One with unlimited energy of mind, heart and soul (Lk 10:27). For the Christian, however, this love is not an indefinite global affection because it is now determined and shaped by the name "Abba." The love of Jesus for God is the particular filial affection for the father; this is the relationship into which he invites his followers when he lets them share his prayer.[9]

Whether God is named in direct, second person address or in third person predication, a specific affection is invoked, a definite way of standing before the Lord is taken. Psalm 23 shows how the affections are schooled. The invocation "The Lord is my shepherd" should *evoke* the very trust expressed in the rest of the doublet: "there is nothing I shall want" (23:1). One can authentically use this image for God only by standing before God in confident surrender, which may at times be either a rich experience or only a dry, deliberate turning to God. Nevertheless, both shepherd and Abba evoke a particular way of standing before the Lord, a disposition and attitude of the heart and will.

What names are appropriate for God and how are they ordered? Here confession of the narrative of salvation becomes the ordering invocation of the affections: doxology is normative for prayer and the dispositions it cultivates. The psalms do not recite God's saving deeds because of some defect in the divine memory; rather the memory that needs to be focused is that of the person or community praying the psalm. The ground of Israel's hope is objective because it is historical. As Israel enters again into that history, the corresponding hope and fidelity are summoned forth. Israel is responsive to that history, that object of its affections.

> O God, our ears have heard,
>> our fathers have declared to us,
> The deeds you did in their days,
>> in days of old:
> How with your own hand you rooted out the nations and plant-
>> ed them. . . .
> For not with their own sword did they conquer the land,
>> nor did their own arm make them victorious,
> But it was your arm and your right hand
>> and the light of your countenance, in your love for them.
> You are my king and my God,
>> who bestowed victories on Jacob (Ps 44:1–5).

Doxology is not an indifferent recital of facts. This confessing prayer is the occasion of renewing those dispositions which the community needs. Doxology engages the believer not only with a single aspect of

God but with the rich character of the God who has acted in history. It evokes a constellation of affections appropriate to the One remembered and praised. The history of Israel and of Jesus are the objective correlatives for the affections of the believer and consequently should exclude mere projection, any fabrication of a convenient deity who fits our desires. Rather, our desires are disciplined or schooled to fit the true God.

Don Saliers, a contemporary American Methodist theologian who writes in the tradition of Jonathan Edwards, describes the formative effect that liturgical prayer has upon the affections. The language of such prayer, he states,

> evokes and educates us in certain specific emotions by ascribing to God what is believed about God, in the vocative mode. Thus in coming to regard God in certain affective patterns, our own personal existence is involved. . . . [By describing the object of our prayer through metaphor and image] our attention and affective intention targets God and, in so doing, it involves those deeper dimensions of the human self expressed in the metaphor of the heart. The language of prayer not only "expresses" emotion in these ways, it forms and critiques the emotional life as well.[10]

We are instructed to "intend" God and the rest of creation in a new way through prayer formed by Scripture, to "stretch toward" these objects and be disposed toward them differently. The names of God and the narrative we confess present very definitely qualified objects to the affections, making them in turn discriminating about what they "intend."

### Patience: A Test Case

Let us consider the affection of patience. Is the patience experienced by the Christian internally different from that experienced by a Stoic? Someone nurtured on the writings of Seneca or Marcus Aurelius would strive to endure the vicissitudes of life with *apatheia,* a form of equanimity that refuses to permit either tragedy or success to upset personal balance. The Stoic intends a distinctive world and adopts a corresponding disposition toward it. If the world is at root impersonal and oblivious to personal destiny and if the individual is only part of the organic whole, then it makes sense to seek to transcend pain with a detached self-transcendence. For the Stoic there is no possible freedom from suffering but there is always the freedom to exit life by rational suicide.[11] Seneca practiced his philosophy with terminal consistency by slitting his wrists when life became unendurable and expiring in a warm bath.

Christian patience is shaped by different objects and disposes one away from suicide. It sees itself as the creation of a benevolent and merciful God. Christian patience is shaped by the memory of Jesus' passion, which leads to a paradoxical victory through God's fidelity and power. A range of metaphors, from the seed that falls to the ground (Jn 12:24) to the conception of Isaac in Sarah's lifeless womb, points to reliance on God, especially in times of utter frustration. A sense of identification with the risen Christ held out to those who share his sufferings adds an element of joy to patient endurance. Saliers writes, "The language which describes the world as God's creation and the arena of divine mercy is related *internally* to the ability to rejoice in all circumstances—even in the midst of suffering. . . . The particularity of Christian joy, then, is in the object of rejoicing."[12]

Suicide violates the dispositions engendered by this complex affection of Christian patience. Such patience would encourage persevering in the convictions of the faith and being nourished by them to abide personal crises and successes. The contrasting attitudes toward self-destruction indicate that Christian patience and Stoic *apatheia* are simply different affections because they are formed and guided by incompatible images and convictions. We do not have the same affection motivated by different reasons—they are simply different affections. As Stanley Hauerwas expresses it, these two affections are "narrative-dependent" because they are defined by different stories about the self and its world. The story is a necessary ingredient in their definition. The exhortation to patient hope in the Letter to the Hebrews shows how meaning and motive are inseparably linked:

> Let us keep our eyes fixed on Jesus, who inspires and perfects our faith. For the sake of the joy which lay before him

he endured the cross, heedless of its shame. He has taken his seat at the right of the throne of God. Remember how he endured the opposition of sinners; hence do not grow despondent or abandon the struggle. In your fight against sin you have not yet resisted to the point of shedding blood (Heb 12:2–4).

Scripture engenders a distinctive set or constellation of affections correlative to its story, which disposes the agent to act in distinctive ways. In *Can Ethics Be Christian?* James M. Gustafson describes how the affections link religious convictions and appropriate moral actions: "Basic is the affirmation that the experience of the reality of God evokes, sustains, and renews certain 'sensibilities' or 'senses,' certain sorts of awareness, certain qualities of the human spirit. These in turn evoke, sustain, and renew moral seriousness and thus provide reasons of the mind and heart for moral life, indeed for a moral life of a qualitatively distinctive sort."[13] Certain moral dispositions correlate with the experiences of God which are named by the images of Scripture; the bridge between them is a specific set of affections. Gustafson cites some of the principal affections so engendered: a sense of radical dependence, of gratitude, repentance, obligation, possibility and direction. Like a balance of forces, they are interdependent and reciprocally defining. For example, repentance without a sense of hope and possibility would not be a fitting response to the reality of God as witnessed in the biblical tradition.

These affections are like elements on a delicately balanced mobile; the framework that keeps them in balanced tension is the overall structure of the story of Israel and Jesus. Specific narrative units define a given affection, such as the woman caught in adultery in John 8, which is instructive for any repentant sinner coming to Christ. The specific history of Jesus taken as a whole provides the dramatic unity for the various qualities of Christian affectivity. Saliers writes, "The essential feature of the order among Christian emotions is that they take God and God's acts as their object and their ground."[14] Remembering and confessing these saving acts schools the affections. Doxology, the language of praise, locates the believer in the rhythm of the history of salvation and evokes the affective dispositions to support a life that will witness to the Lord of that history.

## II.  The Origin of Affections

The experiences that give rise to every affection shape it just as surely as the object the affection is directed toward. Object and origin are closely related because the desired object is in the desire, and the need for this object gives rise to the desire. We will distinguish the two main origins of Christian affections, the memory of having been loved by Christ and the gift of the Holy Spirit. Some ethicists describe the new commandment as moving from indicative to imperative as all biblical morality does. In effect, they argue that the biblical mandate is, "Become what you already are; what has been done for you by God directs you to do the same for others."[15] However, the move from what has been to what should be is not a logical deduction but an affectionate transfer of energy. How does this transfer take place? Scripture testifies to an historical memory of Jesus' love and to the present continuation of that love, the indwelling Holy Spirit. How are these factors present and operative for the Christian today? Do we have only a remote historical memory of the love of Jesus as the norm for our love for one another?

First of all, we must presuppose some human experiences at the origin of any affection, religious or otherwise. For the assertion that God is love to make sense we must take for granted some memories of human love in the one who hears it. If the individual lacks any experience of trustworthy friends or parents, it may be meaningless to call God faithful or constant.[16] Herein may lie the reason that Christian communities should love people in a noticeable and distinctive manner. For those who have no experience of genuine love and concern, the service and love of Christians must provide the initial referent that will make the Gospel meaningful for them. This referent will always be ambiguous because any limited experience is never untainted by human selfishness. Whatever memories of these qualities we presuppose in others must be transformed by the selfless love of Christ. God loves us in ways surprisingly different from the love of others.

### Jesus Christ's Love, Memory and Presence

The memory of Jesus' love may well have guided the first generation of disciples, but how can it function for us so many years later?

We must have some experience of God in our lives, however obscure it may be, that is analogous to the experience of the first disciples. The biblical images are not testifying primarily to long-past events; the audacious claim of faith is that they disclose the same Lord to our own lives. Faith comes through *recognizing* this same God in our lives. The doctrine of the resurrection of Christ arose in the New Testament in part because of the lively consciousness that his Spirit was among his people. To recognize, to disclose, means that a hidden reality is "unveiled"; literally, it is the basis of the word "revealed." This disclosure occurs when our suffering is grasped as somehow meaningful in light of the cross of Christ, or, rather, when the one who hung on the cross has been present in and to our own struggles. Faith comes from gracious hindsight into our own histories, as the disciples fleeing to Emmaus could look back and recognize the stranger who had walked with them (Lk 24:13–35). The memory of that One present in our past empowers confidence that he continues to walk with us in our current obscurity.

The affections are schooled not only by a biblical vocabulary that liturgical prayer uses to address God, but also by biblical scenes that contemplative prayer savors and relishes. Contemplation is the imaginative entry into a particular scene; every story becomes my story. I identify in mind and heart with the adulterous and repentant David, the irrepressible Bartimaeus who insists on being cured, the swagger and fear of Peter hearing of the impending passion of Jesus. By identifying with their experience based on similar ones of my own, I am also able to identify with their reactions to the words of the Lord—they are spoken to me, too. This is the opposite of play-acting; their cries, prayers and laments turn out to be the most authentic words to voice my own experience. Without this imaginative identification we are but distant spectators of people's lives, and no revelation occurs in our own lives. (Perhaps no class of believers runs this risk more directly than professional theologians and biblical scholars. Ironically, the critical distance necessary for their exegesis can become an unbridgeable gulf between them and the Word of God. What is required is the "second naiveté" described by Paul Ricouer: to return to the text to participate in it, enhanced but not crippled by critical thought.[17])

Without this touchstone in people's religious experience, they have little, if any, capacity to grasp biblical morality, the call hidden in the gift. Does it do any good to spell out the Gospel's demands to those who have never experienced the Gospel itself? Without memory, a different mandate will be heard. As Karl Rahner writes, "Where someone has not had an initial experience of God and of his Spirit, liberating him from his deepest fears and from guilt, there is no point in announcing the moral norms of Christianity to him. He would not be able to understand them; at best, they might seem to him to be the source of still more radical constraints and still deeper fears."[18] Hearing the preached word or contemplating the written word of Scripture may be the occasion for this liberation from fear and guilt. Scripture can provide images that illuminate previous events so that God's presence is disclosed to us in our past, even if it was hidden at the time.

Sometimes we need to be shocked into recognizing God's presence in our situation. The prophets attempted to goad Israel into a felt appreciation of its true state before the Lord, a task Walter Brueggemann describes as "the ministry of prophetic imagination." Jeremiah fashions symbols and broadcasts his own grief to break through the numbness of his times and expose its self-deception. Brueggemann states, "I believe that the proper idiom for the prophet in cutting through the royal numbness and denial is the *language of grief,* the rhetoric that engages the community in mourning for a funeral they do not want to admit. It is indeed their own funeral."[19] Only those ready to grieve can actually perceive what state Israel is in: the affection becomes the vehicle for the truth. Even from a distance of many centuries, believers can enter into that prophetic grief for their own world, and it can disclose for them God's own anguish today over injustice and the incurable wound of the people (Jer 11:17–22).

The author of Isaiah 40—60 uses a different literary genre to incite a different affection in the dispirited people of the exile. Whereas Jeremiah had used the poetry of lament, this writer breaks into lyric song and doxology. "Why, O Jacob, do you say, and declare, O Israel, 'My way is hidden from the Lord, and my right is disregarded by my God?' " (Is 40:27). God has been with them even in exile, and, based on this joyful recognition, Deutero-Isaiah encourages the exiles to anticipate their own homecoming. It will be a second exodus, a triumphant delivery from slavery. Brueggemann writes, "I believe that rightly embraced there is no more subversive or prophetic idiom than the practice of doxology which sets us before the reality of God, of God right at the center of a scene from which we presumed he had fled. Indeed, the language of amazement is the ultimate energizer in Israel. . . ."[20] If we can imaginatively and affectively enter into the lyric of the prophet, we may recognize the same Lord in our own time of exile. The symbols and poetry that inspired hope in his listeners can energize subsequent generations who believe in the one Lord of history.

## *Gratitude: The Path from Memory to Action*

Gratitude is the central affection that moves us from faith memory to corresponding action. It makes the memory an empowering source of moral generosity; it recognizes that the gift of God requires us to act generously toward others. The Reformers inveighed against a morality based on expectation of reward, and rightly so: such self-interested effort destroys gratitude and hence undermines the basis of Christian morality. Just as earning your own keep is the exact opposite of responding to a freely given gift, so too the moral lives based on these two approaches are simply incompatible.

Bruno Schüller contends that the new commandment of John 13 is an instance of the golden rule: it appeals to a basic sense of fairness and self-consistency in us. We should love others because we prefer to be treated in like manner. The indicative of God's gift moves us to the imperative by a logical consistency reminiscent of Kant's categorical imperative. This, however, seems inadequate; a sense of fairness may evoke justice but it does not evoke love. The love God has shown us in Christ was a merciful attitude directed toward those who were alienated. Gratitude for unexpected gifts evokes a corresponding merciful love toward others, especially those most distant from us and those most in need.

The parable of the unjust steward illustrates the central role played by gratitude. The steward makes no transition from the mercy he has been shown to his treatment of his fellow servant. He has been forgiven the staggering amount he embezzled, which would have been impossible to repay, but he turns around and abuses another servant who owes him a minor sum. The king is outraged not at the steward's inconsistency but at his monstrous ingratitude. There is no comparison between the two debts, and such a great gift of forgiveness should have inspired life-altering gratitude. Love should have engendered love and forgiveness should have led to more forgiveness out of gratitude; love does not engender love out of self-consistency (see Lk 16:1–8).

All of the moral imperatives of the Bible are authorized and energized by this gratitude for such undeserved mercy and love. James Gustafson comments on the biblical maxim, "Freely you have received, freely give." He writes, "The comma, in a sense, covers the fulcrum of a way of life. In its affective dimensions, the sense of gratitude moves the will to act. . . . It is out of a sense of gratitude that both moral volition and an imperative arise. God has freely given life to us; we, in thankfulness to him, are to be concerned for others' well-being as he has been concerned for ours."[21] Our memories of grace are not complacent. They incite moral action because gratitude enables us to see what they imply—that we are now required to do likewise—and also empowers us to do it.

No single formal principle can do justice to the rich variety of biblical morality, a variety rooted in the plural theologies and literary forms found in the canon. Nevertheless, one formula may indicate the unity of Gospel and law, of gift and call that pervades all the writings. Imitation of God and imitation of Christ is the most comprehensive form of scriptural morality: "Be holy as I am, says the Lord" in Old Testament language; "Your attitude must be that of Christ" in the New (Phil 2:5). Love responds to an energizing action that instructs and empowers its actions. This imitation is not external. As Gustafson explains, "The form is more like: 'God has done *a, b,* and *c* for the well-being of the human community and the whole of creation; those who have experienced the reality of God's *a, b,* and *c* are moved and required to do similar things for others.' "[22] This formulation points back to the particular history of the individual and the tradition that has revealed the distinctive ways of God. These become both motive and norm for a distinctive moral response from those who have been so loved and forgiven. "Go and do likewise" sums up this morality of imitation.

## The Spirit of Jesus

The Holy Spirit is the second ingredient that functions as the origin of Christian affections. Even though this has rarely been a locus of clear theological exposition, the gift of the indwelling Spirit is presented by the New Testament writers as an important source of moral life. The Fathers of the Church described this union between the Christian and the Spirit as a "participation" in the life of God. Here we can present only some biblical basis for the thesis that the imitation of Christ stems from this participation and that the Spirit of Jesus forms the affections in a distinctive way.

In the Pauline writings the role of the Spirit in human transformation and ministry is intriguing but unclear. The ambiguity lies in *pneuma,* which variously refers to the divine presence of the Holy Spirit and to the new dimension of the person that is introduced by the presence of the Spirit, as in "spirit" contrasted with "flesh." In Romans 8 we find the two usages blending together. Despite the confusion of terms, Paul is undoubtedly asserting a new dynamic that will guide and empower the convert over the old dynamic of sin and the flesh. "The law of the spirit," he writes, "the spirit of life in Christ Jesus, has freed you from the law of sin and death. . . . But you are not in the flesh; you are in the spirit, since the Spirit of God dwells in you. . . . All who are led by the Spirit of God are sons of God" (8:2, 9, 14). This Spirit directs their prayer from within as it enables them to call God "Abba" and wait in hope for their deliverance.

This new dimension of life produces characteristic qualities in the person, the "fruits of the spirit," which are opposed to the "works of the flesh" that divide and pit people against each other. Paul describes these new dynamics that unify the community and build it up. The "spirit" dimension of the life of the converts should direct the selfless way of life rooted in Christ:

> In contrast, the fruit of the spirit is love, joy, peace, patient endurance, kindness, generosity, faith, mildness, and chastity. Against such there is no law! Those who belong to Christ Jesus have crucified their flesh with its passion and

desires. Since we live by the spirit, let us follow the spirit's lead (Gal 5:22–25).

Thus is the translation of the New American Bible. The Revised Standard Version capitalizes "spirit," locating it in each use as the divine presence rather than an aspect of the person.

Paul does not always refer this participation in the divine life to the Spirit. He exults, "The life I live now is not my own; Christ is living in me" (Gal 2:20). In Philippians, he indicates a further source of power and encouragement within the Christian: "It is God who, in his good will toward you, begets in you any measure of desire or achievement" (2:13). In the same letter he writes that he draws the capacity to rejoice even in suffering from "the support I receive from the spirit of Jesus Christ" (1:19). In 2 Corinthians he states that he and other mature Christians do not judge by the worldly standards that the immature Corinthians use; they interpret things with the aid of God's Spirit. He then sums up this new principle by asserting, "We have the mind of Christ" (2:12–16). Finally, it is the Spirit who assigns each one his or her appropriate role in the body of Christ and supplies the love that ought to animate and unify the community. The least we can conclude from this range of references is that Paul experienced a divine directive force from within and expected his audience to have similar experiences. How this indwelling presence of God works together with the human faculties of the individual is left unexplained. But such ambiguity should not lead us to ignore these rich hints at participation in the life of God, Jesus and the Spirit as a basic source of Christian living.

The Gospels of Luke and John expand on this gift of the Spirit as a personal guiding force in the post-resurrection community. The gift of the Spirit on Pentecost seems to effect for the disciples what the baptism of Jesus with its gift of the Spirit effected for Jesus. It launches public ministry with a messianic anointing: the sick are healed, blind people have sight restored, the Gospel is proclaimed fearlessly. The Spirit leads the apostles into the same confrontation with the Jerusalem establishment and persecution that Jesus endured. As Acts proceeds, the Spirit intervenes at crucial junctures to guide the revelation of the Gospel to the Gentiles and bring it to Rome through Paul's ministry.

In John's last discourse in chapters 14 to 16, Jesus promises that the Advocate will replace him in the disciples' experience: "The Paraclete, the Holy Spirit, whom the Father will send in my name, will instruct you in everything, and remind you of all that I told you" (Jn 14:24). In the climactic moment when Jesus is lifted up on the cross to draw all to himself, the act of dying is the simultaneous expiration of this Spirit on the world. On the night of the resurrection, the Lord appears to the frightened disciples and inaugurates them into his own mission of reconciliation and witness by breathing the Spirit on them (20:22–23). When examined in light of the vine and branches analogy, it becomes clearer that their witness will be not so much an imitation of the Master's example as a participation in the continuously fruitful life of Jesus.

## The Spirit: Origin of Christian Affections

Jonathan Edwards referred to the Holy Spirit as the "principle" or point of origin for all the gracious affections. There is a correlation between the distinctive affections the Spirit facilitates in the Christian and the virtuous affections of the historical Jesus. Edwards maintains that one sign of truly Christian affections is that "they naturally beget and promote such a spirit of love, meekness, quietness, forgiveness and mercy, as appeared in Christ."[23] In all the diversity of individual personalities, some common identity is being fashioned in the dispositions so that 'there is grace in Christians' answering to grace in Christ, such an answerableness as there is between the wax and the seal; there is character for character: such kinds of graces, such a spirit and temper, the same things that belong to Christ's character, belong to theirs."[24] Edwards concludes that there is a normative correlation between the dispositions of Christ and those of the Christian because the Spirit of Jesus has been given to them as the source of these dispositions.

Recent biblical scholarship has confirmed Edwards' insight about the role of the Holy Spirit in forming the Christian after the pattern of Jesus Christ. James D. G. Dunn analyzes Paul's use of the historical Jesus as the definition of the Spirit. He writes, "This means that in Paul's view the Spirit has been limited or has limited himself in accord with the yardstick of Jesus. *The power of God has become determined by its relation to Jesus.*"[25] The risen Christ is experienced

as Spirit by the believing community, and, conversely, the Spirit of
God is now experienced as Christ. Only because the Spirit has taken
on the character of Christ can the Spirit create the character of
Christ in believers. Dunn captures the union of Jesus and the Spirit
by describing Jesus as "the personality of the Spirit."[26] He ties this
Pauline teaching together with John's pneumatology:

> Two comments must be made: first, in relating the Spirit to
> Jesus in this way John is doing what Paul did: *John's "other
> Paraclete" is Paul's "Spirit of Jesus."* For John as for Paul
> the Spirit has ceased to be an impersonal divine power; the
> experience of new life alone does not sufficiently character-
> ize the activity of the Spirit (3:5–8; 4:10–14; 6:63; 7:37ff.;
> 20:22). The Spirit has taken on a fuller or more precise
> character—the character of Jesus . . . so, the Spirit of reve-
> lation has been brought into conjunction with the heavenly
> Jesus and bears the stamp of his personality. Second, the
> importance of this equation is that it affords *an immediate
> and direct continuity between believers and Jesus.*[27]

The early Christians saw themselves in continuity with the disciples
of Jesus by this link of the Spirit. They were conscious of being
formed by the same Spirit as the early disciples, and through that
Spirit were present to the vitality of the risen Lord who retains the
character of the historical Jesus. The person of the historical Jesus
and the values he embodied could as a result be the criterion of char-
ismatic experience. They could ask, "Is the Spirit of Jesus here?"

Jerome Murphy-O'Connor, O.P. stresses the Christian community as the primary locus of the Spirit of Jesus. The transformation of
individuals occurs in and through their incorporation into the local
instance of the body of Christ. Ephesians 4 stresses that the "new humanity" being formed in the world is identical with the communal
Christ. As a whole, the community is called to image forth God's reality. "As the community deepens its commitment to the ideal, the
existential attitude of Christ (cf. Phil 2:5) becomes progressively
more manifest, primarily in the community and derivatively in the
individuals who constitute it. To the extent that the community ex-
emplifies the authentic humanity manifested by Christ, it judges

from the standpoint of Christ. It is in this sense that it can be said to possess 'the mind of Christ.' "[28] The community internalizes the values of Christ through the Spirit of Jesus so that, as it matures, it judges according to the fundamental norm of Christian morality, the person of Jesus Christ. To the extent that the community is faithful to the Spirit, it mediates to the individuals who compose it this "mind of Christ" as normative for their own formation of character and moral decisions.

The origins of the Christian's affections, then, correspond to the objects of the affections, which refer both to the historical Jesus and the story of Israel. The images Scripture uses as the names of God disclose the true significance of Christians' own histories: they have been loved by Christ and that love becomes both the motive and the norm for their morality. Out of gratitude they are empowered and required to "go and do likewise." This responding love inextricably links motivation and meaning: the moral imperative is not fully understandable apart from the historical action of Jesus which continues to be present through the Spirit. Imitation evolves out of participation, out of the depths of the community the Holy Spirit dwells in, guiding it toward the appropriate way of following Christ. Even the individual's sufferings deepen the life of faith because of the validation the Spirit provides:

> We even boast of our afflictions! We know that affliction makes for endurance, and endurance for tested virtue, and tested virtue for hope. And this hope will not leave us disappointed, because the love of God has been poured out in our hearts through the Holy Spirit who has been given to us (Rom 5:3–5).

When we expand our conception of what is normative, we discover a way in which the life of Christ as presented in the Scripture can be a norm for Christian living. Norms are not only general principles or moral values that have been abstracted from the story of Jesus and then reapplied in the lives of his followers. (This remains part of the task of Christian ethics: to specify the meaning of Gospel non-violence, poverty, compassion, etc. in an intellectually clear fashion.) In the more concrete regions of the heart, a different sort of norm emerges. The memory of the whole life of Jesus and the story of God's dealings with Israel provide a norm for Christian affections. The story schools the affections, shaping a discerning heart that can perceive the moral response that is appropriate. Actions that are incompatible with this story will clash with the affections of the mature Christian; they will be ruled out because of this felt inconsistency, not primarily because of logical incompatiblity with abstract moral norms. Hence, the object of Christian affections, the One toward whom they stretch, functions as a norm for Christian moral discernment.

Christian affections not only stretch in a definite direction, they also come from a definite source. The Christian through the body of Christ is inspired by the Spirit of Jesus. The New Testament does not confine this inspiration to direct commands of God but even more refers to the Spirit a "person-forming" role, a gradual transformation of the dispositions and intentions of the person which has traditionally been termed sanctification. This person-forming process also is guided by a norm: the life of Jesus whose Spirit has been poured out in them. The fundamental norm of Christian ethics then is the person of Jesus Christ. Growth in Christian life is nothing less than conformity to Christ, a conformity which emerges from within the person and the community. Imitation of Christ comes from participation in the Spirit of Jesus.

Obligation becomes a personal matter, a form of *noblesse oblige* for those who have been joined to Christ. Its binding force originates in personal loyalty and gratitude that compel to service. One cannot directly command affections, but one can be obedient to the patterns of moral action that may occasion deepening of compassion, service and commitment to justice. Finally, even these patterns must be tested against the criterion for this way of life which is nothing less than an actual historical life.

# Epilogue

Why are theologians saying such different things about Scripture and ethics? In part the answer is that they are only reflecting the rich diversity of the canonical text itself, the wealth of literary forms and vehicles found in both Testaments. A more general answer lies in the variety of methods which these theologians bring to bear on Scripture. "Method" is literally the "way" that an argument is constructed, the strategy that organizes the parts into a coherent whole.

There are three main ingredients of theological method that have surfaced in our review. The role of Christ in morality, the type of ethics preferred and the particular theologian's understanding of the Bible as revelation are crucial factors in the method of Christian ethics. The disagreements on using Scripture stem from the different positions taken on Christ, ethics and revelation. Does Jesus Christ endorse ordinary human morality or does he set a distinctive agenda for his followers? Is ethics largely a matter of rules and deeds that determine our duty, or is ethics primarily character formation where actions flow from deep dispositions? Finally, is the Bible revelatory only of the consciousness of the first generation of Christians or does it reveal a living Word that inspires believers directly in every epoch? No argument in Christian ethics can proceed coherently without taking a stance on such questions.

If we change our position on Christ, ethics, or Scripture, it will affect our conception of the other two. Christian ethics is more like a baroque fugue with interwoven themes and rich counterpoint than the single melody line of folk music. Changing one theme recasts the others. For example, Yoder's understanding of the cross as a politi-

129

cal execution stamps his Christology and his ethics and his selection
of biblical materials. Only radical discipleship that is obedient to
God in non-violent resistance is consistent with the person of the
Master.


## Who Do You Say That I Am?

Jesus' provocative question to the disciples can also be posed to
the theologian. Who Christ is will modify the ethics that is employed
because the adjective "Christian" modifies the noun "ethics." These
lines of influence also travel in the opposite direction since the type
of ethics preferred by the theologian may determine what role Christ
plays in moral experience. What Bonhoeffer wrote applies to every
formulation of Christian ethics, namely that the person of Jesus
Christ stands between the disciple and the command. Christology interprets the moral command.

There are several different understandings of who Christ is in
the New Testament. Paul focused on the central event of the cross
and resurrection and virtually ignored Jesus' public life. Luke does
not denigrate the passion narrative, but he fleshes out the picture of
Jesus' attitudes toward women, the poor, and those beyond the pale
of Israel. In 2 Corinthians 8, the Jesrusalem collection is an opportunity to express the mind of Jesus: "How for your sake he made himself poor though he was rich, so that you might become rich by his
poverty" (v. 9). The idealized community of Acts 2:42–47 and
4:32–37 shares its goods in imitation of the compassion shown by the
Spirit-anointed Messiah of Luke's Gospel. The same moral mandate
of material generosity is reinterpreted according to the Christologies
of Paul and Luke, bringing different motives to bear on sharing of
goods.

How can we portray the interaction of ethics and Christology?
James Gustafson's classic work *Christ and the Moral Life*[1] offers a
helpful framework. Gustafson notes that we speak about morality on
four different levels. The most concrete level of moral discourse is
the *expressive* language which registers our approval or scorn for persons or actions. The *moral* level goes a step beyond this by providing
specific reasons or guidelines to explain our moral judgments. The
*ethical* level is more general than the "moral" one because it pro-

vides some of the theory that backs up the particular rules. We cite general moral principles such as justice or charity and theories of character when challenged about our practical guidelines and values. Finally, the most general foundations for our moral commitments are *post-ethical*, "after or beyond ethics." These are our fundamental beliefs about what is ultimately worthwhile, about nature and God. Gustafson shows that most major theologians have concentrated on one of these levels of moral discourse and adopted a Christology that corresponded to that preferred level.

## Foundational Beliefs

Karl Barth primarily discussed the "post-ethical" level of morality. In a way, he had no other choice since he had dismissed both moral rules and general theories of ethics on theological grounds. For Barth, Jesus is "the Lord who is Creator and Redeemer."[2] This is the Christ who stands between disciple and command, and who interprets the moral mandate. Barth can be a frustrating partner in moral discourse because he insists on giving theological answers to moral questions. Why should I do X? Not because moral principles or consequences justify X but because X will witness some aspect of the reality of God, will correspond to the theological realities expressed in doctrines. God's command will always be Gospel before law because it reflects the divine reality in which sovereign graciousness always comes first. The reader who wants moral or ethical reasons from Barth must be braced for a scolding. Attention to ethics means one desires reason to justify one's existence, not Jesus Christ. Ethics, in brief, is sinful! Nevertheless, Barth seems willing to provide general norms for action when he gets down to questions of life and death. In part, this represents his retreat from philosophical existentialism that saw moral rules as a refuge from authentic, free decision.

## Ethics: Transformation of the Agent

The majority of theologians we considered concentrated on the ethical level of discourse. Jesus Christ was presented not as a moral teacher but as one who transformed the moral agent, giving a new heart and mind which would lead to renewed conduct. Jesus Christ is the Justifier and the Sanctifier, the one who transforms the depths of self-understanding and motivation, who proclaims a new reality and not just a new way to act.[3]

H. Richard Niebuhr and Stanley Hauerwas present a portrait of Jesus that corresponds to this ethics of transformation. Jesus is the key to a new self-understanding that operates through a distinctive moral character. For Niebuhr, one can only be actively loyal to the cause of Christ (universal reconciliation) by first faithfully interpreting experience through the "symbolic form" of Christ. Jesus sought to be universally responsible to the action of God, even in the absurdity of suffering and rejection. Jesus becomes the "Rosetta stone" for Christians to search out the traces of the one God who acts in the multiple events and relationships of their lives. He helps Christians to a new self-understanding by unveiling the meaning of their histories, thus evoking new levels of loyalty and trust in God.

Hauerwas fleshes out Niebuhr's rather abstract Christology by developing the narrative of Jesus. This more concrete portrait of Jesus provides a more definite ethics of character. Christ provides a normative story for the Christian, a lived pattern of meaning that can enable the Christian to face life truthfully. "Character" is self-understanding become dynamic, making action integral with one's deepest commitments. The person of Jesus is the Kingdom come, the truth about God's way of acting in the world. That truth is learned through the living witness of the Church and is embodied in the distinctive Christian virtues that reshape the agent's character.

Liberation theology and the revised Catholic moral theology also concentrate on the transformation of the agent. In both schools of thought, ethics has a great influence on Christology. Karl Rahner's theory of the human person as defined by acceptance or denial of God's self-communication lies behind the work of Fuchs and Schüller and most moral theologians today. At the core of our humanity is self-defining freedom that is confronted with the mystery of God. Christ is the one human being who can reveal the promise of humanity and enable us to respond fully to the offer of grace.

Gutierrez also has a theory of ethics; it is based, however, on economic and social analysis rather than on Rahnerian categories.

Christ continues the liberating work of God in history; he is the new Moses, the liberator of the poor. Only those who have opted for the oppressed can grasp the significance of Jesus.

Both schools offer an ethics that can be a bridge to those in the culture who are not Christians. They are deliberately non-sectarian. Neither wants to consign the leaven of the Gospel to a Christian ghetto. Anyone of good will should recognize the truth of their ethics and can understand the validity of the moral arguments they make. Corresponding to this moral vision, Jesus Christ is not presented by them as a sign of contradiction to the non-believer. Christ embraces humanity's true worth and makes possible a truly human existence, which for the liberationists must include struggling to throw off the forces of domination. When we move from the level of ethics to the practical moral application, the similarity between liberation theology and moral theology disappears. The post-Vatican II moralists move from theory to practice by using a variety of sophisticated methods. They have continued the traditional emphasis on getting down to cases ("casuistry") by using natural law, consequentialist, personalist and Kantian modes of reasoning. On the other hand, many liberationists seem to go from their commitments to practice without passing through ethics. Gutierrez' utopian view of the "new man" is so vague that it is unable to provide a normative view of human action. One is left with a situation ethics that intuits what should be done by identifying with the immediate needs of the oppressed.[4]

The summary position we called "responsive love" also concentrates on the ethical level of moral discourse. It too pays greater attention to the moral agent than to the moral act. From the gradual transformation of the agent's affections we can expect Christian conduct to flow "naturally." Ethics draws its power from aesthetics in this view because the attractive power of Christ's person moves the Christian to appropriate action. Duty is grounded in beauty.

What role do moral rules play in this ethics of Christian affectivity? They are definitely not the source of moral conduct, because there can be no imperatives to produce affections. The deep commitments of the heart are evoked by their objects, the qualities of God revealed in history; they are also nourished by the Spirit of Jesus within the person. Affections can guide the moral agent to interpret rules and apply them with that sensitivity we call discernment. In sum, imitation of Christ comes out of participation in God's love rather than by inference from norms.

## Practical Morality

Contemporary Christian ethics does not use the Bible as a sourcebook of moral norms. Most of the authors we investigated propose an illuminative rather than a prescriptive use of Scripture. Decisions should be made in light of the central concerns and commitments of the canonical text, but decisions are not directly derived from biblical prescriptions. The Christian draws direction and a basic orientation from biblical faith. Other sources of moral wisdom, including moral philosophy and appropriate empirical data, are needed to determine the proper course of action.

Barth and Bonhoeffer showed considerable confidence that the individual Christian would recognize the command of God. They do not offer us much insight on how we hear this immediate mandate. We are told that difficulties in hearing God's command are rooted in sinful reluctance to obey, not in some breakdown of moral reasoning. If we had a set of clear moral norms, wouldn't they turn into a new form of "law" that could undermine the free grace of the Gospel?

John Howard Yoder emerged as the most insistent advocate for fidelity to the actual moral norms of the Gospel. For Yoder, Jesus had a definite social ethics which his followers must obey in their time. That ethic of non-violent resistance finds support in Yoder's Christology: the crucifixion was a political execution of a threatening non-conformist. In *The Original Revolution* and other works, Yoder re-examines both Old and New Testament passages to argue that their moral appeals are still pertinent for believers in our day.[5]

The practical level of morality is the one that received the least attention in the authors surveyed. In part, this was due to the theoretical intentions of the works: they were not primarily addressing specific moral problems. A more fundamental issue lies in the authority which biblical imperatives have for the Church today. Most of the moral questions that challenge us today have no counterpart in biblical times; hence there are no specific biblical norms that can be cited. Second, the problem of cultural relativism is a major twentieth century issue in interpreting the biblical text.

The abundant critical work that has been done in this century to establish the cultural setting of the canonical texts has made one conclusion inescapable: first century Judea is radically different from our world. How do we move across that cultural distance—or should we even attempt to do so?

Most theologians who employ the Bible today consider it to be the normative statement of Christian identity. Whatever additional moral insight we derive from ethics or the social sciences must be tested against the portrait of God and of Christ found in Scripture. Jesus did not, however, proclaim simply a moral message; rather, he announced an event, the breaking in of the reign of God. Most theologians would agree with James Gustafson that Scripture does not present a revealed morality but a revealed reality.[6] The theologian must find ways of describing that reality so that moral insight can be gained for responding to God's action.

The problem of cultural distance between our era and biblical times has stimulated theologians to seek the underlying concerns and commitments of the Word of God that still apply. They have turned to a wider range of literature in the canon to find elements that express these enduring challenges—to story and symbol, to prophetic rhetoric and apocalyptic, to parable and doctrinal exposition. Something may get lost in the process. New attention needs to be given to biblical imperatives because moral imperatives play an indispensable part in reflective living. Also, the procedures by which their reflection moves from symbol or story to application need to be clarified.

Moral development studies recognize the role of rules in forming the character of young people. We need to practice some forms of behavior in order to gain insight into their value. Humane behavior is not only the expression of virtues; it is usually also their foundation. The merciful will obtain mercy because they know what it looks like; the arrogant and vengeful will be blind to the mercy that God offers them. The imperatives of the Gospel have a radical quality that forces us to consider the distance our ordinary motives have from the novelty of the Kingdom. The prohibition on divorce, the admonition to turn the other cheek, the mandate to invite the down-and-out to our dinner parties call us to acknowledge the gap between our ways and God's ways. They have an eminently practical religious impact which can be diluted if they are rephrased in more abstract terms.

These practical mandates are radical because the gift of God in Christ is radical. They connect the Christian with the historical person of Jesus Christ and the specific way of life that remains a surprise and a scandal. David Tracy describes the effect on Christian moral reflection that this challenge of the historical Jesus produces:

> The memory of Jesus confronts all sentimentalized notions of love with the intensified extremity of the actual thing in the remembered life of Jesus of Nazareth: compassion and conflict; preference for the outcasts, the poor, the oppressed; love of the enemy; love as hard other-regard that looks to the strength of the kind of love present in Jesus' ministry, expressed in his cross, vindicated by God in his resurrection; love as a freedom for the other that comes as gift and command from the strength of God to disallow the resentful weakness of the too-familiar caricatures of that love as mere "niceness."[7]

The most promising element of the renewed interest of theology in using Scripture for moral reflection is this return to the vitality of God's revelation. As more attention is given to the practical imperatives of Scripture, the unique call contained in the particular gift of Jesus of Nazareth may better school our hearts and deeds. This call to a distinctive way of life, these scandalous requirements, reveal the depth of God's empowerment in the gift of his love. Foundational theological truths and the moral understanding of the agent provide the context to interpret these practical requirements, but to grasp the gift we finally have to hear and act upon the gracious call contained in the gift of God.

# Notes

## Introduction

1. John Howard Yoder, *The Politics of Jesus* (Grand Rapids: Wm. Eerdmans Publishing Co., 1972), p. 80.

2. Martin Luther, *The Large Catechism in Christian Ethics,* ed. by Waldo Beach and H. Richard Niebuhr, 2nd ed. (New York: John Wiley and Sons, 1973), p. 254.

3. John Macquarrie, *Three Issues in Ethics* (New York: Harper and Row, Publishers, 1970), p. 91.

4. "Decree on Priestly Formation," *The Documents of Vatican II,* ed. by Walter M. Abbott (New York: Guild Press, 1966), p. 452.

5. Bernard Häring, *The Law of Christ,* 3 vols. (Westminster: Newman Press, 1966); Joseph Fuchs, S.J. *Natural Law: A Theological Investigation* (New York: Sheed and Ward, 1965).

6. See *Norm and Context in Christian Ethics* ed. by Gene H. Outka and Paul Ramsey (New York: Charles Scribner's Sons, 1968); Paul Ramsey, *Deeds and Rules in Christian Ethics* (New York: Charles Scribner's Sons, 1967).

7. Thomas Aquinas, *Summa Theologiae,* IIIae, q. 106, a. 1.

8. Joseph Fuchs, *Human Values and Christian Morality* (Dublin: Gill and Macmillan Ltd., 1970), p. 122.

9. See Gustavo Gutierrez, *A Theology of Liberation* (Maryknoll: Orbis, 1973), p. 276.

10. H. Richard Niebuhr, "Is God in the War?" *Christian Century 59* (1942):953-55.

11. Stanley Hauerwas, *A Community of Character* (Notre Dame: Univ. of Notre Dame Press, 1981), pp. 212–29.

## Chapter 1

1. Dietrich Bonhoeffer, *Letters and Papers from Prison,* ed. by Eberhard Bethge, (New York: The Macmillan Co., 1967).

2. D. Bonhoeffer, *The Cost of Discipleship* (New York: Macmillan Publishing Co., 1963), p. 99.

3. Martin Luther, "The Freedom of a Christian," in *Martin Luther: Selections from His Writings,* ed. by John Dillenberger (Garden City, New York: Doubleday and Co., 1961), p. 76.

4. Bonhoeffer, *Discipleship,* p. 47.

5. Ibid., p. 63.

6. Ibid., p. 88.

7. Ibid., p. 69.

8. See James M. Gustafson, *Christ and the Moral Life* (New York: Harper and Row Publishers, 1968).

9. Bonhoeffer, *Discipleship,* p. 96.

10. D. Bonhoeffer, *Ethics,* ed. by Eberhard Bethge (New York: The Macmillan Co., 1955), pp. 50–51.

11. Bonhoeffer, *Discipleship,* p. 250.

12. Rudolf Bultmann, *Jesus and the Word* (New York: Charles Scribner's Sons, 1958), p. 103.

13. Ibid., p. 52.

14. Ibid., p. 129.

15. Ibid., p. 77.

16. Ibid., p. 92.

17. Eberhard Busch, *Karl Barth: His Life from Letters and Autobiographical Texts* (Philadelphia: Fortress Press, 1976), p. 87.

18. Karl Barth, *Epistle to the Romans* (London: Oxford University Press, 1960).

19. Karl Barth, *Church Dogmatics* II/2, ed. by G.W. Bromiley and T.F. Torrance (Edinburgh: T. and T. Clark, 1957), p. 557.

20. Ibid., p. 676 (my emphasis added).

21. Ibid., p. 584.

22. Ibid., p. 585.

23. Ibid., p. 586.

24. Ibid., p. 574.

25. Ibid., p. 577.

26. Ibid., p. 609.

27. Ibid., p. 618.

28. Ibid., p. 686.

29. Ibid., p. 682.

30. Ibid., p. 687.

31. Ibid., p. 697.

32. Karl Barth, *Church Dogmatics* III/4, ed. by G.W. Bromiley and T.F. Torrance (Edinburgh: T. and T. Clark, 1961), p. 407.

33. Ibid., p. 331.

34. Ibid., p. 339.

35. Ibid., p. 412.

36. Ibid., p. 421.

37. Ibid., p. 430.

38. Ibid., p. 449.

39. Karl Barth, *Church Dogmatics* IV/2, ed. by G.W. Bromiley and T.F. Torrance (Edinburgh: T. and T. Clark, 1958), pp. 533–613.

## Chapter 2

1. John Macquarrie, *Three Issues in Ethics,* p. 91.

2. See A.P. d'Entreves, *Natural Law* (London: Hutchinson University Library, 1970), ch. 4.

3. Thomas Aquinas, *Summa Theologiae* I-IIae, Ques. 91, art. 1; Ques. 93.

4. Ibid., Ques. 106, art. 1.

5. Bernard Häring, *The Law of Christ,* 3 vols. (Westminster, Md.: The Newman Press, 1961–66); *Free and Faithful in Christ,* vol. 1, (New York: Seabury, 1978).

6. National Conference of Catholic Bishops, "The Challenge of Peace: God's Promise and Our Response," *Origins,* vol. 13, no. 1 (May 19, 1983), pp. 4–19.

7. Josef Fuchs, S.J., *Natural Law: A Theological Investigation* (New York: Sheed and Ward, 1965).

8. Ibid., p. 20.

9. Ibid., p. 63.

10. Ibid., p. 17.

11. Ibid., p. 74.

12. Ibid., p. 75.

13. Ibid., p. 34. See Karl Barth, *Church Dogmatics* III/4, p. 215.

14. J. Fuchs, *Natural Law,* p. 132.

15. Josef Fuchs, S.J., *Human Values and Christian Morality* (Dublin: Gill and Macmillan Ltd., 1970) chs. 1 and 2.

16. Op. cit.

17. Josef Fuchs, S.J., "Is There a Specifically Christian Morality?" in

*Readings in Moral Theology No. 2* ed. by Charles E. Curran and Richard A. McCormick, S.J. (New York: Paulist Press, 1980), pp. 10–11.

18. Thomas Aquinas, *Summa Theologiae* I-IIae, Ques. 106–14.

19. J. Fuchs, *Human Values,* p. 100.

20. J. Fuchs, "Is There?" p. 15.

21. Karl Rahner, S.J., *Theological Investigations,* vol. 6, ch. 13, "Theology of Freedom" (New York: Seabury Press, 1974).

22. J. Fuchs, "Is There?" p. 10.

23. Karl Rahner, S.J., *Theological Investigations,* vol. 5, ch. 17, "The 'Commandment' of Love in Relation to the Other Commandments" (Baltimore: Helicon Press, 1966).

24. J. Fuchs, *Human Values,* p. 122.

25. J. Fuchs, "Is There?" p. 12.

26. Ibid.

27. Bruno Schüller, S.J., "The Debate on the Specific Character of a Christian Ethics: Some Remarks," in *Readings in Moral Theology No. 2* ed. by Curran and McCormick, p. 216.

28. Ibid., p. 210.

29. Bruno Schüller, S.J., "Can Moral Theology Ignore Natural Law?" *Theology Digest,* vol. XV, no. 2 (Summer 1967), p. 97.

## Chapter 3

1. Gustavo Gutierrez, *A Theology of Liberation* (Maryknoll, N.Y.: Orbis Books, 1973).

2. Letty M. Russell, *Human Liberation in a Feminist Perspective—A Theology* (Philadelphia: Westminster Press, 1974).

3. Phyllis Trible, *God and the Rhetoric of Sexuality* (Philadelphia: Fortress Press, 1978).

4. G. Gutierrez, "Notes for a Theology of Liberation," *Theological Studies* 31 (1970), pp. 244–45.

5. Gutierrez, *Theology of Liberation,* p. 49.

6. Avery Dulles, "The Meaning of Faith Considered in Relationship to Justice," in *The Faith That Does Justice,* ed. by John C. Haughey (New York: Paulist Press, 1977), p. 13.

7. Gutierrez, *Theology of Liberation,* p. 205.

8. Ibid., p. 37.

9. Ibid., pp. 157–58.

10. Ibid., p. 159.

11. Ibid., p. 162.

12. Ibid., p. 167.

13. Ibid., p. 175.
14. Ibid., p. 176.
15. Ibid., p. 195.
16. Ibid., p. 202.
17. José Miranda, *Marx and the Bible* (Maryknoll, N.Y.: Orbis Books, 1974), pp. 58–72.
18. J.H. Yoder, *Politics of Jesus*, p. 239.
19. Walter Rauschenbusch, *Christianizing the Social Order* (New York: Macmillan, 1912).
20. Gutierrez, *Theology of Liberation*, p. 176.
21. Ibid.
22. Ibid., p. 276.
23. Leonardo Boff, "Salvation in Jesus Christ and the Process of Liberation," in *The Mystical and Political Dimension of the Christian Faith*, ed. by Claude Geffré and Gustavo Gutierrez, *Concilium* 96 (New York: Herder and Herder, 1974), p. 89.
24. Juan Luis Segundo, S.J., *The Liberation of Theology* (Maryknoll, N.Y.: Orbis Books, 1976), p. 116.
25. Gutierrez, *Theology of Liberation*, p. 203.
26. Ibid., p. 208.
27. Trible, *God and Rhetoric*, p. 202.
28. Russell, *Human Liberation*, p. 58.
29. Ibid., p. 138.
30. Ibid., p. 34.
31. Trible, *God and Rhetoric*, p. 21.
32. Russell, *Human Liberation*, p. 152.
33. Ibid., p. 141.
34. Ibid., p. 156.
35. Trible, *God and Rhetoric*, p. 161.
36. Ibid., p. 196.

## Chapter 4

1. Bruce C. Birch and Larry L. Rasmussen, *The Predicament of the Prosperous* (Philadelphia: Westminster, 1978).
2. Charles E. Curran, *Themes in Fundamental Moral Theology* (Notre Dame: Univ. of Notre Dame Press, 1977), pp. 136–38.
3. See H. Richard Niebuhr, *The Responsible Self* (New York: Harper and Row, 1963), Chapter 1.
4. H. Richard Niebuhr, "War as the Judgment of God," *Christian*

*Century* 59 (1942): pp. 630–33; "Is God in the War?" ibid., pp. 953–955; "War as Crucifixion," ibid. 60 (1943), pp. 513–15.

5. H.R. Niebuhr, "Judgment," p. 630.

6. H. Richard Niebuhr, *The Meaning of Revelation* (New York: The Macmillan Co., 1960), p. 63.

7. Ibid., pp. 63–64.

8. H.R. Niebuhr, "Judgment," p. 631.

9. H.R. Niebuhr, "Crucifixion," p. 515.

10. H.R. Niebuhr, *Meaning of Revelation,* p. 113.

11. H.R. Niebuhr, *Responsible Self,* p. 165.

12. Ibid., p. 155.

13. H.R. Niebuhr, "Is God in the War?" p. 954.

14. H.R. Niebuhr, *Meaning of Revelation,* p. 79.

15. Ibid., p. 79.

16. Ibid., pp. 88–89.

17. Ibid., p. 74.

18. Ibid., p. 138.

19. Ibid., p. 97.

20. Ibid., p. 129.

21. See James M. Gustafson, *Can Ethics Be Christian?* (Chicago: Univ. of Chicago Press, 1975) pp. 130–43.

22. H.R. Niebuhr, *Meaning of Revelation,* p. 73.

23. Birch and Rasmussen, *Predicament of the Prosperous,* p. 73.

24. Ibid., p. 85.

25. Ibid., p. 102.

26. Ibid., p. 113.

27. Avery Dulles, *A Church To Believe In* (New York: Crossroad, 1982), pp. 8–9.

## Chapter 5

1. Charles M. Sheldon, *In His Steps* (Chicago: Moody Press, 1956).

2. David Tracy, *The Analogical Imagination* (New York: Crossroad, 1981), Chapters 6 and 7.

3. H.R. Niebuhr, *Meaning of Revelation,* Chapter II, "The Story of Our Life."

4. George W. Stroup, *The Promise of Narrative Theology* (Atlanta: John Knox Press, 1981), p. 194.

5. Stanley Hauerwas, *A Community of Character* (Notre Dame: Univ. of Notre Dame Press, 1981), p. 6.

6. Ibid., p. 66.

7. Ibid., p. 48.
8. Loc. cit.
9. Ibid., p. 70.
10. Ibid., p. 128.
11. Stanley Hauerwas, *Truthfulness and Tragedy* (Notre Dame: Univ. of Notre Dame Press, 1977), p. 24.
12. Ibid., p. 35.
13. Ibid., p. 33.
14. Ibid., p. 91.
15. Ibid., p. 93.
16. Ibid., p. 90.
17. Ibid., p. 95.
18. Sallie McFague, *Speaking in Parables* (Philadelphia: Fortress Press, 1975), p. 157.
19. Ibid., pp. 32–33.
20. Ibid., p. 1.
21. Ibid., p. 36.
22. J.H. Yoder, *The Politics of Jesus,* p. 99.
23. Ibid., p. 97.
24. Ibid., p. 239.
25. Ibid., p. 238.

## Chapter 6

1. See Jer 32:31–34; Ez 36:24–29.
2. See Gerhard von Rad, *Old Testament Theology* (New York: Harper and Row, 1962), Vol. 1, p. 199; James M. Gustafson, *Can Ethics Be Christian?* (Chicago: University of Chicago Press, 1975); *idem, Ethics from a Theocentric Perspective* (Chicago: University of Chicago Press, 1981).
3. Raymond E. Brown, *The Gospel According to John* (Garden City N.Y.: Doubleday, 1970), Vol. II, *The Anchor Bible,* Vol. 29A, pp. cxxxviii, cxxxix.
4. Bruno Schüller, "The Debate on the Specific Character of a Christian Ethics: Some Remarks," in *Readings in Moral Theology No. 2,* ed. by Charles E. Curran and Richard A. McCormick, S.J. (New York: Paulist Press, 1980), p. 213.
5. H. Richard Niebuhr, *Meaning of Revelation,* p. 70.
6. Ibid., p. 72.
7. Jonathan Edwards, *Religious Affections,* ed. by John E. Smith, *The Works of Jonathan Edwards,* Vol. 2 (New Haven: Yale University Press, 1959), p. 95.

8. C.S. Lewis, *Surprised by Joy* (New York: Harcourt Brace Jovanovich, 1955), p. 220.

9. James D.G. Dunn, *Jesus and the Spirit* (London: SCM Press Ltd, 1975), pp. 21–37, 308–326.

10. Don E. Saliers, *The Soul in Paraphrase* (New York: Seabury Press, 1980), p. 29.

11. Seneca, "On Suicide," in *Ethical Choice*, ed. by Robert N. Beck and John B. Orr (New York: The Free Press, 1970), p. 53.

12. Saliers, *Soul in Paraphrase*, pp. 66–67.

13. J.M. Gustafson, *Can Ethics Be Christian?* p. 92.

14. Saliers, *Soul in Paraphrase*, p. 13.

15. See Victor Paul Furnish, *Theology and Ethics in Paul* (Nashville: Abingdon Press, 1968), p. 225.

16. See J.M. Gustafson, *Theocentric Perspective*, pp. 196–209.

17. See Paul Ricouer, *The Symbolism of Evil* (Boston: Beacon Press, 1967), pp. 19–24.

18. Karl Rahner, S.J., *The Shape of the Church To Come* (London: S.P.C.K., 1972), pp. 66–67.

19. Walter Brueggemann, *The Prophetic Imagination* (Philadelphia: Fortress Press, 1978), p. 51.

20. Ibid., pp. 69–70.

21. J.M. Gustafson, *Can Ethics Be Christian?* p. 101.

22. Ibid., p. 115.

23. J. Edwards, *Religious Affections*, p. 345.

24. Ibid., p. 347.

25. J. Dunn, *Jesus and the Spirit*, p. 319.

26. Ibid., p. 325.

27. Ibid., p. 351.

28. Jerome Murphy-O'Connor, O.P., *Becoming Human Together* (Wilmington, Del.: Michael Glazier, Inc., 1982), p. 214.

## Epilogue

1. James M. Gustafson, *Christ and the Moral Life* (New York: Harper & Row, 1968).

2. Ibid., Chapter II.

3. Ibid., Chapters III and IV.

4. See Gustavo Gutierrez, *The Power of the Poor in History* (Maryknoll, N.Y.: Orbis Books, 1983) for a collection of his essays since 1969 that attempts to specify his practical proposals.

5. John Howard Yoder, *The Original Revolution* (Scottdale, Pa.: Herald Press, 1971).

6. James M. Gustafson, "The Place of Scripture in Ethics: A Methodological Study," in *Theology and Christian Ethics* (Philadelphia: Pilgrim Press, 1974), p. 121.

7. David Tracy, *The Analogical Imagination* (New York: Crossroad, 1981), p. 330.

# Suggested Readings

## A. General Works on Biblical Ethics

Bartlett, David, *The Shape of Biblical Authority* (Philadelphia: Fortress, 1983).

Birch, Bruce C., and Rasmussen, Larry L., *Bible and Ethics in the Christian Life* (Minneapolis: Augsburg, 1976).

Furnish, Victor Paul, *Theology and Ethics in Paul* (Nashville: Abingdon, 1968); *The Moral Teaching of Paul* (Nashville, Abingdon, 1979).

Houlden, J. L., *Ethics and the New Testament* (New York: Oxford University Press, 1977).

Mott, Stephen Charles, *Biblical Ethics and Social Change* (New York: Oxford University Press, 1982).

## B. Scripture and the Revised Natural Law Tradition

Curran, Charles E., *Themes in Fundamental Moral Theology* (Notre Dame: Notre Dame Press, 1977).

Fuchs, S.J., Josef, *Personal Responsibility and Christian Morality* (Washington, D.C.: Georgetown University Press, 1983).

O'Connell, Timothy E., *Principles for a Catholic Morality,* Chapters 3, 11–13 (New York: Seabury, 1978).

Schnackenburg, Rudolf, *The Moral Teaching of the New Testament* (New York: Herder and Herder, 1971).

## C. Liberation Ethics

Crosby, O.F.M. Cap., Michael H., *Spirituality of the Beatitudes* (Maryknoll: Orbis, 1981).

Geffré, Claude, and Gutierrez, Gustavo, eds., *The Mystical and Political Dimension of Christian Faith, Concilium* 96 (New York: Herder and Herder, 1974).

Gutierrez, Gustavo, *The Power of the Poor in History* (Maryknoll, N.Y.: Orbis, 1983).

Miranda, José, *Communism in the Bible* (Maryknoll: Orbis, 1982).

Nolan, Albert, *Jesus Before Christianity* (Maryknoll: Orbis, 1978).

## D. Biblical Symbols and Response

Brueggemann, Walter, *The Land* (Philadelphia: Fortress, 1977).

Johnson, Luke T., *Sharing Possessions: Mandate and Symbol of Faith* (Philadelphia: Fortress, 1981).

Priestley, Denise, *Bringing Forth in Hope: Being Creative in a Nuclear Age* (New York: Paulist Press, 1983).

## E. Parable and Narrative Ethics

Jeremias, Joachim, *The Parables of Jesus* (New York: Scribner's Sons, 1963).

Lambrecht, S.J., Jan, *Once More Astonished: The Parables of Jesus* (New York: Crossroad, 1981).

McClendon, Jr., James Wm., *Biography as Theology* (Nashville: Abingdon, 1974).

Navone, John, *Toward a Theology of Story* (Slough, England: St. Paul Publications, 1977).

Perkins, Pheme, *Hearing the Parables of Jesus* (New York: Paulist Press, 1981).

Shea, John, *Stories of God* (Chicago: St. Thomas More, 1978).

## F. Normative Morality in the Bible

Harrelson, Walter, *The Ten Commandments and Human Rights* (Philadelphia: Fortress, 1980).

Minear, Paul S., *Commands of Christ* (Nashville: Abingdon, 1972).

Perkins, Pheme, *Love Commands in the New Testament* (New York: Paulist Press, 1982).

## G. Conversion and Responding Love

Haughton, Rosemary, *Act of Love* (Philadelphia: Lippincott, 1968); *The Passionate God* (New York: Paulist Press, 1981).

Häring, Bernard, *Free and Faithful in Christ,* Vol. 1 (New York: Seabury, 1978).

Hellwig, Monika K., *Jesus: The Compassion of God* (Wilmington: Michael Glazier, 1983).

Murphy-O'Connor, O.P., Jerome, *Becoming Human Together: The Pastoral Anthropology of St. Paul* (Wilmington, Del.: Michael Glazier, 1982).

von Hildebrand, Dietrich, *Transformation in Christ* (Garden City, N.Y.: Image Books, 1963).

*Other Books in this Series*

What are they saying about Mysticism? *by Harvey D. Egan, S.J.*
What are they saying about Christ and World Religions?
    *by Lucien Richard, O.M.I.*
What are they saying about the Trinity? *by Joseph A. Bracken, S.J.*
What are they saying about non-Christian Faith?
    *by Denise Lardner Carmody*
What are they saying about Christian-Jewish Relations?
    *by John T. Pawlikowski*
What are they saying about the Resurrection? *by Gerald O'Collins*
What are they saying about Creation? *by Zachary Hayes, O.F.M.*
What are they saying about the Prophets? *by David P. Reid, SS.CC.*
What are they saying about Moral Norms? *by Richard M. Gula, S.S.*
What are they saying about Death and Christian Hope?
    *by Monika Hellwig*
What are they saying about Sexual Morality? *by James P. Hanigan*
What are they saying about Jesus? *by Gerald O'Collins*
What are they saying about Dogma? *by William E. Reiser, S.J.*
What are they saying about Luke and Acts?
    *by Robert J. Karris, O.F.M.*
What are they saying about Peace and War? *by Thomas A. Shannon*
What are they saying about Papal Primacy?
    *by J. Michael Miller, C.S.B.*
What are they saying about Matthew? *by Donald Senior, C.P.*
What are they saying about the End of the World?
    *by Zachary Hayes, O.F.M.*
What are they saying about the Grace of Christ?
    *by Brian O. McDermott, S.J.*
What are they saying about Wisdom Literature?
    *by Dianne Bergant, C.S.A.*
What are they saying about Biblical Archaeology?
    *by Leslie J. Hoppe, O.F.M.*
What are they saying about Mary? *by Anthony J. Tambasco*
What are they saying about the social setting of the New Testament?
    *by Carolyn Osiek, R.S.C.J.*